The Living Decalogue, From Sinai to Zion

THE LIVING DECALOGUE

FROM SINAI TO ZION

BY

W. J. COLVILLE

AUTHOR OF

"Old and New Psychology," "The Law of
Correspondences Applied to Healing," "Destiny
Fulfilled—Fate Conquered," "Text Books of
Mental Therapeutics," &c., &c.

THE AUSTIN PUBLISHING CO.
ROCHESTER, N. Y.

INTRODUCTION

The following series of twelve lectures are published at the earnest request of students and audiences in various parts of America, also in England and Australia, who have kindly expressed themselves as desirous that these simple, practical expositions of the Ten Commandments in their spiritual as well as their literal aspects, should be given a wide circulation in permanent and portable form.

Readers are requested to bear in mind that the subject treated is not intentionally dealt with in any critical temper, nor is any claim made that the treatment of the theme is such as to throw any special light on those phases of biblical history and teaching which are now exciting agitation in controversial circles.

As the ethical aspects of the Decalogue are far more important than the historical; and, moreover, as the former can be tested and applied in daily life and rendered serviceable in relation to hourly necessities, while the latter can only afford scope for scholarly investigation, these suggestive essays are confidently presented to the populace with earnest hope mingled with sure expectancy that as the spoken word has been already found helpful, the printed report may prove even more valuable.

No attempt has been made to exhaust the inexhaustible, but the following objects have been clearly present before the mental vision of the writer: (1) To enforce the salutary doctrine of the universality and endless continuity of divine relation and inspiration. (2) To reply in no uncertain manner to those superficial readers of the Decalogue and its traditional surroundings, who claim that The Ten Commandments are anything less or other than a safe and sure repository of universal truth. (3) To detach attention from the merely literal circumstances of an allegorical and poetic narrative, and open out as far as possible in brief suggestive language some of those rich interior meanings which lie deep below the surface of the outward text.

Finally let it be stated, that no attempt whatever has been made to force conclusions on the reader. This volume is the child of conviction, not of dogmatism, and it is sent forth into the world solely to arouse thought, to deepen faith, to counteract needless skepticism and most of all to assist the many who are bewildered because of the jargon of contentious discussions around them and are honestly seeking for some reasonable view of continuous revelation.

The personal experience of the writer leads to the following uncompromising affirmation: The more we search into the Decalogue the more we shall appreciate the deep and lasting hold it has taken upon all civilized humanity, and the more we seek to live by it the more we shall love and honor it.

W. J. COLVILLE.

Christmas, 1904.

LECTURE ONE.

THE APPROACH TO SINAI.

An Enquiry into the Nature and Method of Divine Revelation. The Eternal Basis of Moral Law.

When Matthew Arnold declared that in days to come much that is in the Bible would be gratefully accepted and highly cherished which in his earthly lifetime was being ruthlessly discarded by intellectual iconoclasts, because the discovery would then have been made that the flowing language of poetry, not the rigidly exact language of science, had been employed by the writers, he voiced a prophecy which is now being steadily fulfilled.

The Bible is foolishly assailed by blind literalists who seem utterly incapable of appreciating the sublimity of Oriental prose with its magnificent poetic imagery, but the assaults now being hurled against the venerable Book are largely consequent upon the slavish idolatry of the letter which even yet prevails, though to a constantly modifying extent, among those ultra-conservatives in strictly orthodox camps, who act as though there could be no security for faith or morals if their own crude adoration of local incidents should be relinquished by the masses.

Whoever dares to announce convictions must be willing to oppose and be opposed by two distinct phases of narrow mindedness, the one agnostic or materialistic, the other bigotedly ecclesiastical. Fearless thinkers can afford to remain serene in the midst of all controversies, and today's prophets, like those of olden time, must proclaim the life-giving spirit of continuous revelation despite every obstacle which ignorance and prejudice may throw in their path. *"The letter killeth but the spirit giveth life,"* is a saying true forever.

We attempt in this series of consecutive addresses an investigation of two mountains, and, strange to say, one is within the other. Sinai is the body; Zion is the soul.

The true children of Israel are neither Jews exclusively nor Gentiles exclusively. They are all personalities everywhere who are in process of enlightenment and regeneration. Egypt is a figure of the sense-life of humanity; Canaan is a type of the spiritual estate to which humanity can and will attain, but only by means of a process which we may fairly call evolution —the evolution of involved potencies.

. Revelations are continuous, but human discoveries are not necessarily so without intermissions. There are crises in our lives, days and hours of peculiar significance, and these are periods of judgment. Let none say that because nature's processes are unchanging, that there are no climaxes and no sudden disclosures Whoever would argue thus has never contemplated natural phenomena nor is he at all versed in the science of Geology.

The external aspects of existence with which we are all superficially familiar illustrate precisely the inner workings of spiritual force. Law and order are one. Whoever would understand the working out of divine purpose in human affairs must grasp and hold the supreme thought of universal unity. Our appeal to the entire world can be reasonably based upon the incontrovertible assertion that all the greatest teachers of the human race have dealt in natural metaphors and taught the multitude in parables.

Whoever devoutly and intelligently studies Nature discovers God, but whoever takes to Nature his prejudice or his conceit receives back only the echo of his own opinions. The foolish one says in his heart, "There is no God," and then proclaims that he cannot find the God whom he in the seat of his affections deliberately denies

The idea of God is inborn, but the multifarious doctrines concerning God with which literature is deluged are only so many crystallized limitations of the human intellect.

"God is one and there is no unity like unto the divine Unity." So spake Moses Maimonides, the eminent Jewish philosopher, in the twelfth century, and in these words he did but re-echo the oldest and sublimest thought of God the human mind has ever entertained

All archæological research is proving that behind polytheism stands monotheism, for no matter how many divine revelations there may be, there is but one Supreme Being, and the one only God is beyond human definition.

Genesis truly teaches that human beings are all included in that divine Image which is God's offspring, and Exodus gives a dramatic history of how varying are man's experiences as he seeks to interpret his own containment.

Moses and Aaron are brothers. Aaron is the elder but the weaker; Moses, the younger, is the inspired prophet, while Aaron, the elder, is only the officiating priest. Moses, tho' eighty years of age, when at Horeb he sees the mysterious sight of a bush burning with fire but unconsumed, is a young man ripe for a mission.

Theodore Parker, John Greenleaf Whittier and other illumined modern teachers and poets have sought to universalize this bush, but have permitted it in their commentaries and verses to remain largely a vegetable. That bush in its inmost meaning is Human Nature; nothing more and nothing less.

Moses is an anthropologist, a student of human nature at its highest as well as at its lowest.

Innumerable opportunities are afforded all of us for investigating the crust of human existence; we can all inspect the hide of the human animal, the mere biped who often claims a quadruped for ancestor. But it is given only to the seer, dowered with insight, to peer below this covering and to behold something of the supernal majesty of the divinity within. Happy are they at all times and in all places who turn aside with Moses to see this great sight.

The word of God is Truth, and truth is the only word ever spoken by Deity. This word is spoken out of the flame of fire, out of the inmost of man's own being, for in the soul of humanity is to be found God's dwelling-place. If we desire to be deliverers of our brethren, emancipators of a race from servitude, we must listen with inward ears and gaze with inward eyes, for no outer inspection of ourselves or of our neighbors will convince us that we are other than selfish, sense-bound, even though improved and still improving animals.

We have two distinct consciousnesses, one higher, the other lower. Indubitable testimony to this is being furnished hourly to every one of us through the incontestable medium of our own experience, and in a final reckoning it is never another's theory but always our own experience that proves convincing. We may listen attentively, even reverently, to wise words which fall from the lips of accepted sages of ancient or modern time, but the individual human being must hear a responsive echo within his own breast ere he can intelligently say Amen to another's testimony.

Moses as an individual appears a personality concerning whom much scholarly doubt may be expressed, while the traditional account of the Sinaitic Revelation as having been made to Moses by the Supreme Being thirty-four hundred years ago in the Arabian desert, may be freely discounted by rationalistic theologians as well as by that large class of modern thinkers who, though not averse to what they understand by Natural Religion, place no confidence whatever in the testimony of those biblical students who seek to enforce a literal reading of what is obviously poetry. Surely it need not be reiterated that many parts of the Old Testament are of obscure origin as historical documents, nor does it seem necessary to assert for the millionth time that all Oriental teachers depend very largely upon poetic allegories to enforce the moral and spiritual lessons they seek to inculcate.

If a critic of the Decalogue shall say that the Ten Commandments are three times recorded and that the three accounts do not entirely agree, our only answer is that we are not much concerned about the time and manner of their delivery, as our sole vital interest centers in the Spirit, not in the letter, of the Decalogue; and if it be further objected that we do not need to seek either for inspiration or for moral sanction amid the doubtful records of a by-gone age, our reply must be that as at this very hour these Ten Words are the acknowledged basis of enlightened jurisprudence the world over they are by no means antiquated but living, breathing, palpitating forces in the actual life of all civilized and semi-civilized communities today.

It is often said that the Commandments were known long before the period of Moses, if it be admitted that such a personality is historic, and that one by one the scattered elements of the Moral Law came together by an assimilative and cohesive process explicable on the theory of natural moral evolution. Be that as it may, the Ten Decrees are here today and multitudes of church-going people wherever the English tongue is heard, repeat constantly the time-honored petition, "Lord have mercy upon us and write all these thy laws in our hearts we beseech thee," as soon as the reading of the Decalogue is finished.

Revelation need not startle the senses, but it does sometimes enter the citadel of human consciousness through the gateway of exterior suggestion. Every student of Suggestive Therapeutics is becoming increasingly familiar with the beneficial effects of outward means now being constantly employed for the readier enforcement of ideal spiritual propositions. Childlike people, like children, must be accommodated with declarations of truth not only adapted to their understanding, but presented to them in alluring external ways. The important thing always is not, How did the truth reach us or through what channel has it flowed? but has it reached us at all, and are we in any way conscious of its presence within us as a vitalizing and uplifting power?

The three unmistakable means whereby we arrive at truth are:

(1) The way of the corporal senses, which is the lowest and most rudimentary way.

(2) The way of intellectual approach whereby we are led to see the reasonableness and feasibility of what is recommended to us.

(3) The way of interior enlightenment. Sinai in its most external aspects stands in class one. Reasonable appeals to expediency may be placed in class two. Interior illumination belongs in class three, and at that point we reach Zion.

Whether any particular individual or race of people can be successfully reached by one or another of these distinct modes of appeal, depends necessarily upon the degree of development reached by the individual, community, or nation to whom the appeal is being made. We teach the same fundamental verities in kindergartens as in universities, but we cannot adopt precisely identical methods, and we assuredly cannot employ the same text books.

There is no contradiction whatever involved in adapting truth to the comprehension of the scholar, but never should it be regarded as tolerable to tell falsehoods to children and then indulge the spurious plea that as they grow toward maturity they can unlearn the errors forced upon them by parents and teachers in their childish days.

One of the fundamental points of agreement between all ethical teachers is that while all manner of means may be employed in conveying and illustrating truth, undiluted verity is all we dare to call "sincere milk" adapted to infantile digestion. Just as wrongful as it is from a hygienic standpoint to administer sour milk to an infant, so erroneous is it to offer falsehood in any measure for the acceptance of young or old.

We beg all our readers to weigh carefully the following incontestable proposition: Truth is unvarying as to quality, but ever enlarging as to quantity, in our reception of it. Nothing ever changes which is really and substantially true, but the measure of truth perceived at one time is very much less or greater than at another time by the same individual.

The Moses type of man is a glorious study and as a type his superiority to Aaron is immeasurable. Moses is the seer; Aaron is the priest; this accounts for the fact that the one is incorruptible while the other is easily corrupted.

The present time calls for prophets, and he only is a prophet, and she only is a prophetess of the Most

High, who is utterly fearless of consequences while ever loyal to the utmost vision of truth perceived inwardly.

When we study the tale of Moses at Horeb, as he turns aside to see that great sight, the ever-burning but unconsumable bush, which typifies our true humanity, we may well enquire how many have there been in any age, in any country, who have completely turned aside from all else to contemplate an outspread heaven-born vision.

The scientific explorer is always cast in genuine prophetic mold, while the hireling preacher of conventional theology may be a priest after the order of Aaron, perpetually offering similar oblations which can never make the "comers thereunto" perfect.

What is it to turn aside to see? A myriad wonders are outspread on every hand wherever we may be sojourning or traveling, but unless we have the open eye and open ear we know nothing of all the splendors and marvels which surround and adorn our pathway.

It is never simple doubt which leads to knowledge, but quest of fuller truth, even though honest skepticism is infinitely preferable to blind, unreasoning belief, or that lazy credulity which tacitly accepts everything because it is too idle to question anything.

Genuine revelation comes most perfectly to those intrepid and uncompromising men and women who are fearless and philanthropic enough to consider nothing personal as of any great concern when weighed in the scales with general human interest. A very clear light is thrown upon the Moses type of character when we read even cursorily the leading events in the great Egyptian-Hebrew prophet's life history. If not born to the purple, thoroughly trained to it, heir-apparent to the throne of the Pharaohs, this self-consecrated seer was not only tacitly willing but actively wishful to surrender every prospect of personal comfort, ease, and luxury that he might deliver a race of slaves from bondage.

England and America have during the nineteenth century given us many shining examples that such heroic natures do actually exist, and are by no means, as cynics would have us believe, the fanciful creations of the overheated imagination of poets and romantic novelists. Among many brilliant moral stars of the first magnitude the immortal names of John Howard and Florence Nightingale as well as of Abraham Lincoln, Wendell Phillips, William Lloyd Garison, George Thompson, Lucretia Mott, and scores of others less known to universal fame, stand forth conspicuously and every one in this illustrious company can well be pointed to as a gleaming luminary, blazing the road along which troops of coming reformers will be prepared to tread.

Those who work only for the world's applause, or who are eagerly seeking the thanks of those they desire to benefit, would do well to study the career of that ancient prophet of whom it has well been said by pious Israelites, "There has never arisen in Israel a prophet like unto Moses who beheld God's similitude." Times without number have we been called upon to explain such seeming contradictions as the diametrically opposed statements "No man hath seen God at any time" and "none can see God's face and live" with explicit declarations that Moses saw and conversed with God face to face as one man converses with another. Laying aside for the present all secondary interpretations, which involve a discussion of angels and ministering spirits as intermediaries between God in heaven and man on earth, we refer to that word "similitude," which wise Jewish writers have applied advisedly, and in strict accordance with the first chapter of Genesis which declares that generic humanity is in the divine image, not physically, but spiritually.

Revelation and discovery, though not identical, are closely related terms, and are just as near of kin in their application to moral as to astronomical, chemical, or any other special set of scientific experiences.

A star in the heavens has been revolving in its own particular orbit for uncounted millenia of time, contributing its special quota of light and beauty to the universe, but not until it was discovered by an astronomer on earth was its existence revealed to the people on this planet.

God is compared to the great Central Sun of the Universe, shedding rays of love and wisdom, to which solar heat and light according to Swedenborg and other illumined seers and sages directly correspond. Therefore as an analogy it is not presumptuous to institute the following comparison: Certain prepared conditions and instruments for observation are necessary to the science of astronomy; not only must there be a star-gazer, as the old astrologers and astronomers were termed, but telescopes and spectroscopes as well as observatories are necessary to the prosecution of researches amid the glories of the stellar universe. Physically considered God is unknowable, also to the mere intellectualist who seeks to find Deity in such protoplasm as the eminent Professor Tyndall discovered in the common nettle, or some other simple inmate of the vegetable world, but knowable indeed to all who are properly included in the list of those who, because pure in heart, see God with the eye of spiritual discernment.

Moses was one who did precisely what conscience or moral sense dictated, and kept on following the dictates of his highest self regardless of all external consequences. Many of the members of the oppressed race he determined to emancipate were so sunken in slavery that they felt no gratitude toward their heroic champion, but their thankless attitude toward him did not release him or cause him to seek release from a single iota of the tremendous burden of moral responsibility which rested on him; therefore, amid execrations, as well as amid blessings, he went forward to his herculean task, and worked wonder after wonder through the agency of divinely given power which illustrated clearly for all time the exact place of the real line of demarkation between white magic (leucomancy) and black magic (necromancy).

Pharaoh's court magicians were doubtless something more than vulgar charlatans or insincere pretenders to magical attainments. Genuine soothsayers and mighty occultists they may have been, but as the Egypt of their day had sunk into the foulest degradation and every sort of immorality accompanied the prevailing celebration of popular religious rites, these time-serving magicians were Inversive Magi, or, as they are often called in treatises on Occultism, "Brethren of the Shadow."

On the banks of the Nile, during that exciting *tour de force* between these Egyptian soothsayers and Moses and Aaron, the book of Exodus shows us the full limit of the power possessed by the unscrupulous or black magician. Serpents can be converted into rods and rods changed into serpents; water can be vitiated and its appearance made to resemble blood; locusts, flies, lice, frogs and all manner of elementary forms of life can be conjured up and caused to infest the land, not sparing even the King in his private chamber; boils can be brought forth on the bodies of men and cattle, both by Moses and Aaron and by Pharaoh's hired workers of spells and dealers in enchantments. The clear distinction between white magic and black is discovered at the point where some deed of beneficence is called for. Can you heal the stricken populace or can you relieve the sufferings of afflicted animals? Pharaoh's magicians are compelled to answer, No. But when Moses and Aaron are appealed to they can demonstrate their divine gift as healers of all who are afflicted.

Not a single sacred animal dedicated to the gods of Egypt could escape the plagues which visited the land because of the ungodliness and uncleanliness of the people and their rulers; not a priest of Osiris or of Isis was exempt from a share in the wholesale calamity which befell the entire Egyptian nation; but the Children of Israel had light in their dwellings, health in their bodies and safety in their homes despite the wide surrounding desolation.

However much or however little credence should be placed in the letter of this narrative, as describing the actual state of affairs in the Nile country a few thousand years ago, the obvious spiritual interpretation is as follows: Circumstances are not our masters if we have grown superior to their influence over us. We are, however, their submissive servants so long as we remain in the figurative "Egyptian" state of moral darkness, swayed by animal appetites and governed by desire for earthly honors secured no matter how.

During one of our lecture courses in California some years ago, a young man of some prominence in social and business circles, desired us to give our next lecture on a subject of his proposing, and as his request was readily complied with he stood up and said, in stentorian tones greatly to the amusement of a large majority of the listeners, *"No flies on the children of Israel."*

Laughter, applause and a few hisses greeted the announcement of so unusual a subject for discourse, but to the lecturer the suggestion proved a decidedly welcome one, and never had we any better opportunity for elucidating our deep-rooted convictions on much that pertains alike to metaphysics and to Occultism. Our friends can readily believe that no attempt was made by us to extol one race of people at the expense of others, nor to unduly enforce doubtful history based on a literal rendering of a section of the Pentateuch. Proceeding without delay to the heart of the theme suggested, we sought to explain how in the esoteric sense Egyptians and Israelites signify two classes of people, both living in the world today as truly as in any by-gone period; the former being the sense-bound devotees of prevailing servitude, while the latter are all who are awakening to a vital realization of their divine origin, nature and possibilities.

The literal Jewish problem is not an altogether uninteresting or unimportant one, as the remarkable vitality, intelligence and longevity displayed by orthodox Israelites, even when confined in wretched ghettos or exposed to the rampant fires of reasonless persecution, can always furnish Israel Zangwill or any other brilliant descriptive writer with ample material not only for single books, but for entire libraries of instructive and entertaining literature. If it be true, as rumor hath it, that the ultra-reformed modern Jew is falling a prey to consumption, and other Gentile maladies, due not to civilization, but to artificialization, all we have to say is that there are two palpable causes for this regrettable fact: First, the dietary or physiological reason which we commend to the consideration of all health students and hygienists in general. Second (the far more important one from every mataphysical standpoint), unwillingness to remain singular or peculiar from fear of social and other outward consequences. An old tradition tells us that when the Ten Commandments, engraven upon the two tablets of stone, were found lying on the side of Mt. Sinai, the various nations of the earth went up to the tablets in turn and each nation, after having scrutinized their contents, turned away, refusing to lift them, for they were very heavy and their precepts most difficult to obey. When Israel came and inspected them, Israel, unlike the other nations, took them up and carried them away, thereby assuming voluntarily "The yoke of the Torah." Though such a rational fable cannot be said to follow closely the text of the Pentateuch, it throws a strong sidelight upon vastly more than merely a wondrously eventful national and religious history, for it tells us that if any of us are in possession of more than an ordinary measure of truth it is not because of divine favoritism, but by reason of our voluntary assumption of moral responsibilities, or on account of our having in some way qualified ourselves to take a leading position among others as an elect people who are styled "the light of the world," "the salt of the earth," and known by many other exalted designations.

Among modern poets no one has expressed the highest idea of divine revelation as universal rather than tribal or sectional, more fully than Samuel Longfellow, a brother of Henry Wadsworth Longfellow, who is well regarded as among the chief of modern bards. What can be more expressive of the true idea of world-wide illumination, than the exquisite lines of one of Samuel Longfellow's choicest hymns:

"That which came to ancient sages,
　　Greek, Barbarian, Roman, Jew,
Written in the heart's deep pages,
　　Shines today forever new."

Imperfect though this discourse must be (if any regard it as an ambitious attempt to explain so mighty a subject as revelation in its innumerable aspects) considering that the author's object is to provoke further thought far more than to settle elaborate controversies, it may not be amiss to call attention to a few leading features of a rational theory of revelation in general, before passing on to a *seriatim* review of the Ten Commandments, which we propose to consider in the next 10 lectures without any restrictive reference to their supposed miraculous or supernatural origin, regarding them as monitors for today rather than as relics of a time long since departed.

(1) Revelation and discovery are synchronous terms and can not be logically separated when we are engaged in any review of human experiences.

(2) Revelation is not arbitrarily bestowed upon certain chosen people at favored intervals, but comes anywhere at any time to all who are in a receptive attitude of heart or will, and of intellect or understanding.

(3) The foregoing propositions being accepted, it necessarily follows that all chronological and geographical elements can be entirely eliminated from a practical, helpful study of continuous revelation, so that we can profitably and consistently employ text books which throw light on conditions favorable to a reception of revelation, unmindful of their geographical or distinctively historical elements.

(4) Prophets are for today, as for yesterday. Prophecy has far more to do with exhortations to righteous living than with satisfying the curiosity of any who seek to peer into veiled futurity.

With these considerations borne clearly in mind, it will not be difficult to remove our thoughts very largely, if not entirely, from the vantage ground of past history, and turn from the vanished past to the immediate present. Pentecostal outpourings of the Spirit of Truth are just as possible now as in centuries long since fled; but, now as then, we must gather in one spirit with one accord, whether we assemble in a literal city called Jerusalem or anywhere else. The present Zionist Movement, which is attracting great attention, not alone in Jewish circles where the interest naturally chiefly centers, is one of those problematical undertakings which serve to keep alive traditions of the past and at the same time minister to the yearnings of the present.

There are millions of Jews today who fervently pray that restored Israel may become consolidated in a great prosperous nation dwelling in literal Palestine, but there are other millions of Jews who have no desire whatever to leave lands of birth or adoption in Europe, America, South Africa or Australia, where they are citizens in full exercise of every right of citizenship.

Let those who wish to go to Asia Minor flock thither and re-colonize a wonderful historic spot of earth, but Jerusalem and Zion, like Horeb and Sinai, for all peoples signify spiritual states, not geographical localities.

The true fulfillment of all glowing prophecies concerning a new Jerusalem must be spiritual before it can be literal, but a new heaven, which is man's interior condition renewed, may be finally ultimated in a new earth or exterior condition in which peace will reign absolutely triumphant.

LECTURE TWO.

THE FIRST COMMANDMENT.

"Thou shalt have no other God than the Eternal."

Knowing that there are various translations of the First Commandment, and knowing also that there is ample room for discussion as to which translation of the original most closely conforms to the spirit of the Hebrew text, we shall not attempt to quibble over various readings and perplex our fellow-students with needless discussion of higher and lower or broader and narrower views of Deity entertained by people in remote times, or to improve the Ten Words which are said to have been miraculously given. Having for our immediate object a simple, practical elucidation of the spirit, rather than of the letter, of the first of these Ten Commandments, we need simply to remark that whenever we seek to convey the thought of absolute Deity we shall use the term or title Eternal One, but whenever we are dealing with tutelary spirits, ministering angels, and all local and limited conceptions of divinity, we shall adhere to the conventional usage of the terms God and Lord as we find them employed throughout all sacred scriptures.

The ninety-fifth Psalm is an example of this usage, "The Eternal One is a great King above all Gods." This is a clear, definite sentence, while a frequently employed translation, "The Lord is a great King above all Gods," is somewhat ambiguous. The Hebrew word Adonai almost invariably rendered "the Lord" in English, is a substituted word, as no orthodox Israelite will pronounce the name *Jahveh* or Jehovah when reading from the scrolls of the Law. El-Shadai, meaning the Almighty, is a term in frequent use, but the real name of the Supreme Being, according to orthodox Jewish tradition, is not to be pronounced on earth until Messiah comes and speaks it.

Israel Zangwill, whose stories are all replete with historical information, says in one of his shorter novels, "The Turkish Messiah," that only a very few hundred years ago in Europe there arose a supposed Messiah who eventually became a convert to Mohammedanism, and who, during his earlier days long before his apostacy from the Jewish faith, impressively spoke the Divine Name, the awful *Tetragrammaton* of the Kabalah, but no result or phenomenon followed "Sabbatai's" utterance of the great and awful Name, because he was not the true Messiah.

Innumerable superstitions and countless legends cluster around the Unpronounceable Name, among the very commonest of which is the altogether superficial statement that the tutelar divinity of the Hebrew clan, the God of the mountains, refused to give his name to the specially privileged or singularly endowed sensitives among the ancient Israelites with whom he frequently communicated.

We shall not endeavor to refute those external scholars, whose exegetical methods are purely exoteric, and who therefore see nothing below the most external surface of a spiritual revelation, for on the plane upon which they examine the Pentateuch they are certainly measurably correct. Our aim is not to rehash or revamp old stories of tutelary guardians of Israelitish and other clans, but to delve as deeply as possible into the wealthly mine of precious spiritual ore, the entrance to which can be found in the biblical tradition concerning the giving of the Law from Sinai. As it is not certain that Sinai was ever a volcano, the account of its marvelous eruption can be understood far better allegorically than literally. The fire, smoke, lightning, thunder, earthquake and trumpet-blasts are all to be considered correspondently, if the story as revealed in the group of chapters which circle around the twentieth chapter of Exodus is to be applied to the living present. Moses we regard as typical of all men and women everywhere who are found loyal and conscientious beyond all ordinary wont. No beast can be permitted to touch the mountain, for it will die immediately it sets foot upon the burning elevation. This needs no translation for a student of the Mysteries, as every tyro in Occultism knows that what is signified thereby is, that every animal propensity must have been fully subdued and held completely in submission to the operating will of the indwelling spirit, before the neophyte can possibly end his novitiate and take it upon himself to encounter the sublime and terrible ordeal which ever awaits the incipient hierophant.

Moses must go alone through smoke and cloud; he must brave the darkness and be strong to hear the solemn voice which speaks after the commotion of elements has subsided, a voice that waxes stronger and louder with every fresh step the ascending hero takes on his way to the summit of Mt. Sinai.

We do not presume to say how much or how little modern Free Masons understand of this glowing imagery, all of which is exhibited in the various lodges during solmen rites of literal initiation, but whether exalted members of exoteric Masonic fraternities are familiar with inner meanings or not, we are not afraid to announce that there are genuine Gnostics and Hermetists upon earth today who know whereof they speak when they declare that there is a key extant, which may have been long concealed, but never lost, by use of which the soul of the Torah is found reposing in its body.

Whenever the officiating minister in a synagogue uncovers the sacred scroll and holds it up in sight of the assembled congregation, he symbolizes, if he follows the full prescriptions of an orthodox ritual, precisely what esoteric teachers explain concerning the divine law within the outer covering of extraneous legislation.

Every listener can hear the sound of the reader's voice, every reader can pronounce the words which front his eyes, and every scroll-maker can mark the characters correctly on prepared parchment, but only those who hear and see beneath the literal garb have any true or ideal conception of what the story means which recounts the awe-inspiring experiences of Moses as he ascended smoking, trembling Sinai, and received two tables of stone from heaven at the hands of God's angelic messengers.

Doubtless there are multitudes all over the world today who do sincerely worship not simply an anthropomorphic but an exclusively patriotic or tribal divinity. To many people Israel's God is the God of Abraham, Isaac and Jacob and their descendants, but of no one else. Such a conception may be spiritualistic and need not be untrue in limited measure, but it falls immeasurably short of that exalted universal monotheism which does not deny the facts of polytheism whenever a polytheistic system can find facts to support it—but in its impressive grandeur and unique magnificence alone amid all systems of theology and philosophy, calls upon humanity the world over, to acknowledge one only God as Creator and Preserver of the entire human family.

Many people speak of the "beautiful sentiment" of universal brotherhood and sisterhood, but they put all imaginable intellectual obstacles in the way of its outward realization. Among the commonest objections to this sublimely ideal conception of human solidarity, we find a contracted ethnology on the one hand, and an equally contracted theology on the other. Far be it from our intent to seek to foist upon thinkers in this twentieth century, the utterly unhistoric doctrine that all Jews, three thousand or more years ago, had arrived at the sublimest conceivable view of Deity, and that every man, woman and child among them entertained the idea of a Supreme Spirit absolutely impartial and entirely universal to whom they gave the name of "God of Israel," for such was certainly not the case.

The partially enlightened Hebrew race, which the Jewish religion gradually civilized, had reached no such high pinnacle of ethical or intellectual attainment, and to ninety-nine out of every average hundred of the members of that race, the Jewish God was, no doubt, a being more or less incomprehensible, who watched over the destinies of a "Chosen People," and fought for them against their literal enemies whenever they went forth to battle. But we need not go back three thousand years to find such narrow-minded Jews or similarly narrow-minded Christians, for recent events have abundantly proved that so blind are many vaunting American and English patriots, that to them the words of Decatur, the American general, who said on a memorable occasion in 1816, "My country, right or wrong, always my country," express the highest possible ideal of genuine patriotic sentiment. How much nobler, however, are the words of a wiser general: "My country, right or wrong; if she is right, may I work to keep her right, but if she is wrong, may I use my best endeavors to set her right."

On the foundation of the foregoing for a text, Rev. Samuel Richard Fuller of Boston, a singularly powerful independent preacher, lectured at Greenacre, a charming resort in Maine, July 4, 1899. On that occasion a seven-colored Peace Flag was presented to Miss Sarah J. Farmer, the beloved president of the Greenacre Conferences. In these conferences people of all shades of opinion have, year by year since their inauguration in 1894, taken increasing interest and found increasing benefit by working together despite differences of view regarding many things, for the end of universal peace.

"Have we not all one Father; hath not one God created us all?" was the text or motto of the World's Parliament of Religions held in Chicago during September, 1893. It is worthy of remembrance that this quotation from one of the Hebrew prophets was suggested by Chief Rabbi Adler of Great Britain, and accepted by the Parliament Committee in preference to all others presented. It will never do to confound the highest, deepest, purest, wisest, and most far-reaching teachings of ancient seers and sages with the petty constructions put upon them by merely average intellects. We do ourselves a great injustice as well as proving unfair to our forefathers, if we persist in reading out of ancient Scriptures only the shallowest meanings which superficial thought can gather. Take an artistic illustration: some great painter, sculptor, poet or musician who lived in the long ago, has bequeathed to posterity a priceless gem of art. The ordinary hearer or observer hears or perceives only the most external elements of this masterpiece of painting, statuary or musical composition, and to him the master's *chef d' oeuvre* means no more than some ordinary sketch or concert-hall ballad.

Shall we say that because the common eye sees only the surface of the canvas and the common ear hears only a strange combination of musical notes, that therefore the great artist or composer had no higher conception of the product of his inspired genius than the little the average amusement-seeker attributes to him?

Myriads of literary and art treasures are now being discovered and exhumed, and among the very oldest we find some which compare most favorably with many of the grandest productions of today. In their fierce recoil from blind idolatry of the past and foolish unscholarly bibliolatry, iconoclastic reformers have failed to appreciate the many priceless gems of truth and to discover those profound depths of hidden meaning which our much glorified and also greatly execrated Hebrew Bible contains; but when we note how strong is the influence for good exerted everywhere by its many noble passages, we should have neither right nor reason on our side did we attempt to demolish what only needs to be more fully revealed that it may be vitally appreciated.

Dr. Joseph Parker, author of "The People's Bible," a commentary in twenty-five volumes, often said during the course of his thirty years' ministry in the City

Temple, London, "We do not want a new book, but we do require new readers," to which we can heartily respond, Amen. The new readers, if they are true and profitable ones, must be able to look through the outward dress of an accepted literal revelation and discern its interior strength and beauty. Swedenborgians thoroughly believe in two interior senses below or within the natural sense, which they call the spiritual and the celestial senses, and were these good people freer than most of them appear to be to traverse other fields than the beaten track of Swedenborg's somewhat arbitrary definition of correspondences, they could soon lead the religious world in a very profitable direction; but some of them are sadly handicapped because of their own far too literal rendering of their singularly gifted leader's illuminations.

No writer of ancient or modern date has surpassed Swedenborg in philosophic depth or transcendental grandeur, but the extreme devotion paid by his avowed followers to the literal text of his theological writings has been a decided set-back to the benign influence his entire philosophy is capable of exercising in the world.

God as Supreme Life, Infinite Love and Wisdom, comparable only to a glorious Central Sun, and revealed as Man in Man's inmost essence, is the ancient universal teaching of the Illuminati who are always in the world and ever ready to instruct all who are willing to become faithful, earnest learners in the school of esoteric knowledge, which is essentially a school that seeks to graduate its disciples as quickly as possible, that they may leave the sheltering arms of the Alma Mater who protected their spiritual infancy, and go forth reliant upon the divine life within them, to establish new and ever-widening Schools of the Prophets, in which genuine training shall be afforded all earnest aspirants to a spiritual ministry, entirely at variance with the prescribed scholastic routine to which all conventional priests and rabbis are subjected. It is truly a long spiritual journey from the ritualistic worship prevalent in today's "Egypt" to the sublime spiritual service of the universal Oversoul who is also the Indwelling Spirit, a worship which marks the free "Israelite" who has passed through the wilderness of protracted transitional journeyings and reached the "Canaan" of the soul, the land flowing with measureless supplies of celestial "milk and honey."

There is but one way in which a divine revelation can be tested and perfectly separated from the tare or cockle which grows in the same field with the wheat until the harvest hour of elimination comes.

All man-made systems are ambitious, prelatical, limited, in all ways calculated to unduly exalt some personality, and consequently to consign other personalities equally worthy, well nigh to oblivion.

Let us pass in rapid review some of the present popular systems of thought which are accounted "Advanced," "Liberal," "Progressive," or "New," and see to what a sad extent they are honeycombed with the most ancient error of personal idolatry. Christian Science during the past twenty years has made amazing progress. Churches of Christ (Scientist) are everywhere increasing in membership and influence, and despite the attacks made upon this cult from every side, the young giant waxes ever stronger and more prosperous. With its first breath Christian Science pronounces man the free-born child of God, but with the next the formulated system binds him in old timeworn shackles, limiting officiating ministers to the recitation of stereotyped sermons, and setting up a book, "Science and Health, with Key to the Scriptures," by Mary B. G. Eddy, as an infallible rule of faith and practice. "All is good; there is no evil," is the fundamental sentence at the root of Christian Science doctrine, yet malicious mesmerism and animal magnetism are feared with slavish terror by many who are loudly proclaiming that truth has set them free. There is much of truth in Christian Science, but the entire system is by no means wholly true. It behooves us, therefore, to discriminate intelligently between the truth which it contains and the error with which that truth is mixed. The error springs from failure to trust altogther in omnipotence; half-way confidence in Deity will never emancipate either an individual or a race from bondage.

Theosophy is another modern candidate for worldwide recognition, and not only its name but its claim is truly inspiring; but just as Christian Scientists have idolized Mrs. Eddy, so have Theosophists slavishly bowed to the dictum, not only of Mme. Blavatsky, but of other leaders also, and greatly to the detriment of the Theosophical movement at large. People cannot consistently call upon humanity to subscribe to universal fraternity, and then drift into exclusive Aryanism, nor can they save people from the dangers accruing from misdirected psychic power by fulminating against hypnotism, and sometimes even condemning all phases of mental healing on the ground that it is wrong to interfere with Karma.

Spiritualism is in many respects the most inclusive of all the modern movements, and more and more is the scientific world coming to accept its fundamental claim, but Spiritualists, unsatisfied with legitimate spiritual intercommunication, have insisted upon "spirit control," and consequently have had to reckon with the terror of "obsession." All these weaknesses and causes of strife and unreason take their rise in disobedience to the first commandment, "Thou shalt have no God except the Eternal," and this has been most clearly seen by all the greatest ethical teachers the world has ever known. Though God is absolutely universal, there is a deep sense in which the words of an ancient psalmist, "O God thou art my God," are absolutely true. God, though so far beyond all description that every attempted definition is a vulgar impertinence, must be realized by each human individual as personal to that individual.

We cannot fail to be impressed with a peculiar trick of English speech, which serves to exactly illustrate our finding or our non-discovery of God in the universe. How will you accent the following sentence or how will you punctuate the written phrase? *God is now here.* You would not alter one letter to make it read, God is nowhere. There was a story afloat many years ago that an atheist wrote this sentence on a blackboard and asked his little son to read it. The child read, God is now here. The father intended that it should spell, God is nowhere, but the simple wisdom of the child refuted all his endeavors to inculcate atheism. It may be the better of the two to believe in no God at all,—than to so pervert the thought of God that one might well wish he could live in a Godless universe; but we are forced to no such bitter alternative. Optimism and Pessimism are rival candidates for the people's vote today. Which will you vote for, that inspiring Optimism which finds good in everything, or that depressing Pessimism which finds evil in everything? Choose ye this day whom ye will serve; there can be no further dalliance, no longer a halting between two opinions. "Worship Adonai or worship Baal," said Elijah to the populace of old, and we face today's Carmel even as we front today's Sinai. It is always on a mountain peak that a great revelation is announced to the people. Wonders are not performed in valleys, only on high eminences can we catch glimpses of the Infinite.

The God who answers by fire is the true God today as in all time past. Fire always purifies and enlightens. Does your God-idea enlighten, not only you but the world around you? Are you stronger, braver, purer, wiser and happier because of your faith? If you are not, you are a worshipper of Baal or Baal's successor, Mammon, no matter how loudly you may with the lips profess your faith in the one only true God who is Spirit, and who can be worshiped only in spirit and in truth.

We most of us love only Moriah or we love only Gerizim; we are small Jews or small Samaritans, petty patriots, not large cosmopolites; therefore we are continually looking to externals for what can only be found within ourselves If you are a worshiper on Mt. Gerizim, and nowhere else, you and your Samaritan confreres will soon find that your beloved temple will fall into ruins and leave you templeless, or you will be forced to wander into a distant land and God will be left behind, for you, on the hill of your idolatry, so you will feel as far from God as you are far from home, altar, shrine, or sanctuary. If you are an exclusive worshiper on Mt. Moriah you may live to see a third temple vanish as two temples disappeared before it. How often do we miss all sense of close intercommunion with the divine, because we in our ignorance clutch frantically at some external shrine or object, which, to us embodies all we can as yet conceive of Deity.

Whatever may be the literal history of ancient Israel, or however little Jews in general may have realized the one Eternal Being immeasurably beyond the highest possible ideal of a tribal divinity, we may well be assured that the chief among the prophets everywhere have pointed humanity away from a localized limited God without, to the intimately near God within. No intelligent reader, much less any profound student of the Bible in its entirety, can imagine for an instant that all the various conceptions of Deity to be found on the pages of its many composite manuscripts are but variants of one identical view. Still underlying all smaller views there runs the basic thought of a single Supreme Intelligence whose unity is incomparable, and this view is sustained instead of weakened when we seek to trace the roots of the Hebraic or Mosaic idea of God to Egypt where, notwithstanding the extreme complexity of the popular prevailing polytheism, a rigid monotheistic God-idea was fundamentally established.

The Egyptian "Book of the Dead" contains a long list of minor divinities, and gives a graphic account of the many living creatures of all sorts which the people venerated because they believed them to be in some mysterious manner participants in divine sanctity, but there is absolutely nothing in that strange compendium of old Egyptian beliefs and practices which militates against the theory, now put forward by all the wisest among Egyptologists, that the Egyptians of many thousand years ago conceived of one supreme Deity infinitely above all lesser divinities, and unapproachable save through purification of the human heart and mind. If the Exodus story be accepted in any degree literally, its historic elements connect the giving of the Sinaitic Law with a people recently emancipated from servitude in Egypt, through the agency of a mighty hero, a race deliverer, who had been educated in Egypt at Pharaoh's court and remained in that land until he had completed his eightieth year of age.

The first of the Ten Commandments may, then, be reasonably understood literally to be in the nature of a call to the Israelites to forego all the idolatrous practices of the Egyptians and cling with fervor and sole devotion to all that was truly essential and absolutely noble in their former faith; at the same time they were being counseled to go higher than they had gone hitherto, for yet more stringent rules of morality were enunciated for their guidance than had been revealed to them in all their previous experiences.

The trumpet call from Sinai's height, the special message of the sounding shofar or ram's horn trumpet was, "Hear, O Israel, the Eternal thy God, the Eternal is one;" and "Thou shalt love the Eternal with all thy heart, with all thy soul, with all thy mind and with all thy strength." How significant is the poet-author's statement that the divine voice waxed continually louder and louder, and that only Moses could ascend the mountain and commune with Deity face to face. Leaving all literal aspects of the imposing scene and departing from the pathways of history and tradition, we may profitably ask for the key to the inner significance of the still sounding command, "Worship the Eternal, thy God, Him only shalt thou serve." Nothing can be more self-evident than that with the avalanchine advance of modern liberal religious thought, old opinions concernnig God and revelation have been mightily shaken, and it is equally self-evident that the present epoch is one of unrest, doubtful expectancy and many other transitory elements combined.

We cannot go back, we must go forward. The common idea of God entertained by the credulous fifty or more years ago cannot be reinstated in human consciousness, and it is well for us all that it cannot be. A very urgent enquiry presses itself upon us from every side; are we compelled to give up all that was excellent, comforting and inspiring in our forefathers' idea of Deity, because we cannot accept the result of morbid theological controversies and swallow the contents of creeds, catechisms and confessions which were formulated in obedience to the will of a tyrannical majority, but never voiced the faith of a more spiritually minded minority, whose voice was silenced by the clamor of the verbally victorious party in those ecclesiastical council chambers, where worldly force, rather than spiritual insight, gained the day?

Consider the sage utterances of such great philosophers as Moses Maimonides, who in Europe during the twelfth century expressed himself concerning Deity in the following words: "God is one, but there is no unity like unto the divine unity." "God is pure Spirit and hath no form whatsoever." Such utterances have long been regarded as strictly orthodox among Jews of the most conservative school, and they are certainly not at variance with the pure Theism of Fiske and many other modern writers, who simply tell us that it is all in vain to seek to scan the Infinite. A wise writer has given us the line, "God defined is God dethroned." Nothing can be truer than the above saying, the truthfulness of which impresses us with renewed conviction whenever we are called upon to pass an opinion upon alleged modern revelations, some of which may tell us that people go into trances, travel through seven circles of light and then reach the very centre of the universe and stand locally in the presence of God. There are two explanations of such claims. First, a vision has been mistaken for an actual geographical experience. Second, some sensitive person has seen an angel and imagined that personal spirit of bright and glorious presence to be the absolute ineffable Deity whom no man can possibly behold in any such external manner. The simple ethical import of the First Commandment can well be taken to signify that devotion to the sense of right within is the paramount obligation resting upon us all, and because much dispute hovers about this proposition we will proceed to analyze it.

It is frequently contended that the individual human being cannot be trusted to discover truth for himself, therefore the need of a hierarchy whose infallible dicta must be unquestionably accepted as the supreme rule of faith and conduct. History has proved so conclusively that all hierarchies have been at times corrupt and false, that no fair-minded student of ecclesiastical history can possibly accept the hierarchical claim as well founded. On the other side of the controversy the case is widely different, for instead of intuition or inner light being disregarded by the most enlightened among experimental psychologists, it is now being almost universally conceded that there is a light within every human being endowing each with an adequate though not infinite conception of right or justice. Dr. George Dutton, author of an admirable treatise on Anatomy and many other valuable educational books, has thrown volumes of ethical teaching into a sentence of only six words: *"Justice satisfies everybody; injustice satisfies nobody."* If we take away the latter three we shall find in the three former words alone an all-sufficient basis for every sort of moral educationary work. Does justice satisfy everybody? some will ask. Yes, it does, we uncompromisingly reply. Let the sociologist or political economist travel far and wide in search of a solution of the many complex social and industrial problems now confronting everybody, and he will journey in vain until he dares to announce to the world the great discovery made in every age by every genius, seer or prophet, that all that children ask is justice, and adults are only grown-up children who clamor for the same. It is always a debatable question how far we are justified in releasing all restraints and letting children do exactly as they please; but we are forced at length to meet the issue between worshiping God and honoring one's parents.

The new methods in education—and in these we certainly include the fundamental thought of the Swiss Pestalozzi and the German Froebel—are all based upon the right of a child to live an individual life and grow as flowers grow in a garden; hence the now very popular term Kindergarten (children's garden). Does the First Commandment enjoin upon us these modern views of education? It certainly does, and we cannot obey it ourselves unless we are ready to assist others in their attempts to obey it. Truth must be confessed, even though the confession is often for the time humiliating and therefore unpalatable, and the particular truth we need to confess today is each child's right to individual liberty, which has been so long denied that it seems like anarchy to advocate, in some quarters, obedience to an inborn divine order in place of cringing submission to a tyrannical man-made law.

The First Commandment teaches us to do what is right, because it is right; in place of do as others tell you because they command you. The Decalogue is so searching, it probes so deeply into the very depths of human nature, and is so revolutionary in its effect upon conduct wherever it is obeyed, that multitudes today exceedingly fear and quake when they hear the Ten Words re-delivered from the living Sinai, the mount of God within the very nature of humanity.

How strangely inconsistent we are if on the one hand we glorify those heroic martyrs who submitted to the cruelest persecution rather than effect compromises with conviction, and on the other hand highly extol those very institutionalized practices in opposition to which these same witnesses for truth resisted even unto death. "Let my people go free that they may serve me," and "Where the spirit of the Lord is there is liberty," are two perfectly agreeing texts, one from the Old, the other from the New Testament, which we specially commend to all who are engaged in a study of the essence of the First Commandment. Do we appeal, as we should, to the innate sense of right in the youngest members of our families, and do we enter the secret chambers of our own being often enough with the words in our hearts, "Lord what wilt Thou have me to do?·" How frequently we hear the futile words, "I'll punish you." Probably you will, cogitates the intending transgressor, if you catch me; but, he continues, still parleying with himself, you'll not catch me, therefore I shall go unpunished. Sinai's voice peals in the ears of every human being whenever conscience retorts; but though no man sees you God is all observant and God's ways are not like man's ways. God's penalties are not ulterior, but interior. God does not catch the thief by means of a police and detective service. God does not incarcerate malefactors in dungeons, bind them in chains, and eventually, if they prove incorrigible, hand them over to the executioner.

God works in man through the law of his own nature; therefore all divine rewards and punishments are absolutely inevitable Here appears the solemnity of the entire situation: no one can escape the interior elevation which follows obedience, and none can escape the equally interior and unavoidable deterioration consequent upon disobedience to divine law. We are not called upon to take a look at two literal tables of exterior stone, for the tablets of the Law are within us. One stone table is to be found in the seat of our affections, the other in the citadel of understanding. The Law is written on two tables of stone, not on one table only, because through united will and understanding, through co-operating emotion and intellect, is human life to be rendered harmonious and sublime.

Let us all accompany Moses *into* the mountain as well as *on* to it, and then come forth to perfectly obey the injunction as it concerns all outward behavior, "See thou make all things according to the pattern which God gives unto Moses in the mount."

LECTURE THREE.

THE SECOND COMMANDMENT.

"Thou shalt not make unto thee any graven image."

Probably no one of the Ten Commandments has excited quite so much controversy as this Second Commandment, which not only inveighs against idolatry but introduces the reader to a very decided, though often greatly misunderstood, enunciation of the doctrine of sin and its sequence.

The first part of the commandment which concerns the worship of idols has long been made the subject of controversy, not only between Jews and Christians, or between Christians and Mohammedans, but between Catholics and Protestants, Ritualists and all opposed to Ritualism. It would involve the expenditure of needless and unprofitable effort to seek in this place to re-traverse the long winding road of acrimonious dispute along which controversialists have been treading for many a century; it suffices for our immediate purpose to consider how far we are reasonably called upon to abstain from image making, and at what point we are likely to incur the inevitable penalty which grows out of disobedience to a divine precept.

If the very strictest interpretation of the letter of the commandment be insisted upon, we suppose it would be necessary to agree with the decision of the Græco-Russian Church, that icons or holy pictures are not prohibited, but statues which are clearly graven images, are prohibited by the Law.

The Roman Church long ago decided that only the worship or adoration of images was forbidden, and therefore the Vulgate translation reads: "Thou shalt not bow down to them to adore them," which to the Jewish mind amounts to almost a falsification of the Decalogue, for the Vulgate reading allows people to bow down to images but not to worship them, a distinction real enough in itself but not very easily comprehended by the illiterate.

We think it a fair inference that the spirit of this Second Commandment has nothing whatever to do with the sculptor's art, or with the simple manufacture of statuary; it concerns the attitude taken toward external things in general, rather than in particular. There is a passage elsewhere in the Bible, which throws much light on this discussion: "Idolatry is as the sin of witchcraft."

The Second Commandment forbids all forms of witchcraft, and what are witcheries but results attributed to certain material as well as psychic acts which were always endeavors to cause distress and to bring injury upon people and their belongings. Idolatry in its widest sense signifies all inordinate attachment to material objects; all undue regard for merely external things, and on this branch of the subject we desire to utter some decidedly uncompromising words.

As the present is an age of renaissance in the fullest meaning of the term, for every old and curious practice and belief of days gone by is being revived through the agency of some one or other of the numerous schools of Occultism now extant, we cannot escape confronting in a more or less modernized dress, all forms of ancient sorcery adapted measurably to the taste and demand of these early years of the twentieth century.

There is immeasurable element of truth in all great claims of Mental Scientists and others who insist strenuously upon the sovereign potency of human will and expectation, and go so far as to declare that poverty as well as sickness can be charmed away by purely mental or psychic activity, when such activity is exerted according to law and order.

There is certainly nothing in the Decalogue to dissuade people from setting to work in all possible legitimate ways to accumulate an earthly fortune, and enjoy life in this present (not necessarily evil) world; but one of the essential doctrines of the Wisdom-Religion of all ages is, that we cannot command material resources as long as we take a slavish mental attitude toward them. No servitude is so galling, no serf is so completely enslaved, as whoever makes a god of some material idol and falls down in abject worship before the mental image of some material thing whose outward absence the unhappy idolator continually bemoans.

Before we can cultivate and liberate any psychic force sufficiently to attract to us the things we need, we must be worshippers of God and dominators of Mammon in our own consciences. This is a subject upon which there is a good deal of hazy speculation, and only seldom do we come across a lucid statement concerning the mental attitude truly necessary to govern external supplies.

We cannot serve God and Mammon, but we can serve God and rule Mammon. The service of God can be translated into terms of simple ethics thus: The service of God which is truly described as "perfect freedom," is completely untrammeled obedience to the highest moral conceptions of which we have any consciousness. We serve God when we are true in all respects to whatever we feel to be the right, whether our loyalty to conviction wins for us the praise or blame of our contemporaries.

We must always put right before might, spiritual possessions before material appurtenances; but while this is the order of a well-regulated life it is quite unreasonable to assert that it is God's will that we should live in destitution, or that we must be resigned to circumstances and tamely submissive to untoward environments because we imagine that God has ordained that such should be our lot.

A complete revolution is now in progress in theological circles, the outcome of which will surely be an entire recasting of religious doctrines into the molds of modern speech. Our own sympathies are by no means wholly with conservatives or entirely with radicals, as those titles are commonly employed, because we can plainly see that each party is standing out for some phases of truth which the other fails to perceive. Conservative language is objectionable to radical ears and vice versa, but we must seek to get at an understanding of what we are all alike aiming for, and surely the object of our united aim is the bettering of human conditions in all respects.

Undue regard for material things leads to an immense amount of totally unnecessary crime; therefore it is the duty of lovers of humanity to protest vigorously against a form of idolatry which in the modern world is sapping not only the bodily health, but the moral character of nations. Idolatry is not the simple practice of venerating consecrated shrines or placing flowers and lighted tapers before some much-prized statue, though it cannot be denied that there is a danger that idolatry may supervene if such practices are indulged in an unreasoning manner or to an inordinate degree.

On that side of the subject it is scarcely necessary in these days to do more than exercise rational discrimination between normal and abnormal causes for such devotional practices, and most of all does it become us to treat Oriental systems of religion, such as Buddhism, with the same consideration that many of us are accustomed to show to ceremonial phases of Christianity.

Nothing can be more irrational than to commend in Christendom, practices which we condemn in Heathendom, and certainly all traveled persons, whether their voyages have been only mental or both mental and physical, who have kept themselves free from stupid prejudice while on their journeyings, have reached the decision that there is no more idolatry in setting up an image of Buddha than in erecting a shrine in honor of any saint in the Christian calendar.

The power of suggestion now being exhaustively dealt with in many periodicals to which leading physicians and intelligent people of all professions contribute, is throwing much new light on the origin and meaning of numerous rites which have long appeared barbaric and meaningless to professedly cultivated missionaries who have gone to Eastern countries to turn from "heathen idolatry," people who, in many instances, were far more highly educated and quite as moral as themselves.

The nature of the idea portrayed in the image is a matter of considerable consequence; we cannot afford to deal lightly with the view taken of the image by the worshiper who gazes upon it or bends before it.

Apologists for religious ceremonialism find their case much strengthened by the discoveries of modern psychologists, who are paying great attention to the value of suggestion. All that passes under the name of "Suggestive Therapeutics" throws light on image worship, as it has been vulgarly termed, when viewed as an aid to concentration of thought on a definite ideal. The modern suggestionist is far too inclusive in his appreciation of ceremonial rites to satisfy apologists for any particular phase of religion, for they, unfortunately, seek as a rule to denounce all other systems than their own, while the scientific student and practitioner of experimental psychology embraces all or none. It is not necessary to enlarge further upon this solitary point, but we should be far from making practical application of our theme if we did not use this opportunity to insist upon the crying social need of the present hour, which is that we pay sincere deference to the spirit of the first two commandments of the Decalogue.

The cause of defalcations of every kind is to be found in an utterly vain and foolish idolatry paid to material possessions regardless of how they have been obtained. In all cases where intelligence has been employed in the honest accumulation of material substance, the accumulator is entitled to the sincere respect of the entire community in which he may reside; therefore sound teaching is not at variance with the views of those who laud the honestly wealthy on the score of their superior wisdom.

No one can dispute the saying, "he is a benefactor of the race who causes two blades of grass to grow where formerly but one grew," for such a person adds to the bulk of communal property and is a friend to society at large. There is no rascality involved in honorable engagement in agricultural and mining industries, when those employed in such undertakings are rendering the earth more fruitful and bringing out of its secret places the treasure it has for ages concealed, seeing that no one can be pauperized, but many may be enriched thereby. Let it then not be suggested that people interested in the spiritual development of humanity are in love with financial destitution, and hold up poverty as a sign of piety. Such teaching is utterly erroneous and misleading, at the same time it is intensely necessary to show by example, as well as to proclaim by precept, that we do not value people on account of what they have, but by reason of what they are.

Edward Bellamy, in his two great novels, "Looking Backward" and "Equality," has pointed out with unmistakable clearness that the possession of money affords no proof whatever that it has been honestly obtained, for stolen treasure has the same marketable value as honestly-earned wealth.

It is quite right to show the rising generation that industry and intelligence are passports to honor and the esteem of one's fellows, but these most desirable qualities and qualifications are often conspicuously absent in those who force their way into what is falsely called "the best society," because they hold in their hands a golden key.

Whatever may be said to the contrary, a great increase in material demands is a weariness alike to the intellect and to the flesh, and it was this observation, made long ago by the author of the Book of Ecclesiastes, which made that deeply reflective scribe pronounce the sad verdict, "All is vanity and vexation of spirit," a sentence which does not by any means imply that human life is necessarily vain and vexatious, but only that it is rendered so by the pernicious encouragement of intellectual or sensual idolatry, or a combination of the two. Whatever luxury one feels one cannot do without one needs the discipline of going without; that is why we are so often told by deep reasoners that poverty is sometimes a decided blessing, though at other times it seems an unmitigated curse.

Material things are in their very nature dissoluble or destructible; consequently our tenure of them is, perforce, uncertain. If we have aimed at so high a standard of development or attainment that we rest in the calm assurance that the commanding power is in our own hands, that all material objects are our servants, we being masters over all exterior conditions, we can certainly enjoy fearlessly all the good things of earth which come legitimately in our way; but so long as any of us are in fear of losing what we now hold, our very enjoyment of things—good enough in themselves—is tinctured with dread of their departure; therefore as we are helped by finding out how well we can get along without many things we once regarded as essentials it is often good for us to lose them, so that we may place our health and comfort on a nobler basis.

In these days of rapid and constant transit, travelers are learning more and more the happy art of making material wants as few as possible. Camping out and all varieties of rural enjoyment necessitate bringing material wants into the smallest possible compass, but people do not feel that they are submitting to involuntary deprivation when they feel freer and happier without, than with, a vast array of cumbersome paraphernalia.

Daniel and his three companions at the court of Babylon were not forced, through poverty, to live simply on vegetables and water, but they far preferred their simple fare to all the luxuries of the king's table. Idolatry in thought or in secret affection, worship paid to things we feel forced to go without, is the most pernicious of all phases of idolatry, because it engenders chronic discontent and undermines health and character far more than any ostensible act of commonly acknowledged idolatry. Worship or adoration never really consists in outward acts or in the homage of the lips. Prayer can always be silent and secret, therefore the metaphysical view is the only radical or comprehensive view.

What we love, we draw to us whether we are conscious of this truth or not. For this reason it is always supremely important that we should consider well the direction of our affections before proceeding to employ intellectual machinery to bring the subject of our desires into objective manifestation. Idolatries of all kinds are dangerous, because they cause our energies to flow into profitless, if not into positively mischievous, channels, thereby causing a serious depletion of vital force.

Idolatry causes all sorts of waste of strength, and is responsible for innumerable cases of debility, extremely difficult to account for and still more difficult to cure on simply physiological grounds. Many people are constantly complaining of strange nervous depression, coupled with extreme physical debility, and though they consult physicians, swallow medicines, take change of air and bestow great attention upon the external side of hygiene, they do not recover, but often grow steadily weaker despite all their endeavors to renew their strength.

Interior or subjective phases of idolatry are frequently, if not invariably, responsible for these sad conditions, and the plain-spoken spiritual scientist does not hesitate, in private consultation, to call upon the melancholy invalid to turn his affections as well as his thoughts into new and profitable channels. We are all led by our emotions, affections or sympathies before we are guided by pure reason.

Worship is an impulse of the heart, not a speculation of the brain. We adore what we love, not what we merely believe in. We cannot reduce idolatry to the level of false belief, though false belief may foster and support it. Idolatry takes its rise in the emotions of the heart and enlists the brain to carry out the heart's desires.

We are well aware that modern physiologists may rebuke us for employing the old terminology, and insist that all emotions take their rise in one or other of the three chief divisions of the brain—cerebrum, cerebellum, and medulla oblongata—but however correct may be the present popular physiological definitions, the fact remains that the brain controls all sections of the body in such a way that whenever emotional centres are excited the heart is literally affected either for weal or woe.

All effective healing, which is enduring in its results, enlists the affection as well as the reason of the patient. We can scarcely repeat too often the frequently forgotten truth, that genuine health is, primarily, spiritual and moral elevation, then mental emancipation and improvement, and finally bodily and circumstantial renovation.

The second portion of the Second Commandment containing the well-known words, "I, the Lord thy God, am a jealous God, visiting the iniquity of the fathers upon the children unto the third and fourth generations of them that hate Me, and showing mercy unto thousands of them that love Me and keep My Commandments," is not difficult to understand or to harmonize with the very latest discoveries in the field of heredity, provided we grasp the meaning of the original text.

The word "generations" is a supplied word in the fifth verse of the twentieth chapter of Exodus (King James Version); therefore an erroneous view is taken of the entire passage if it is not supplied in the sixth verse also. The implied *generation*, not *individual*, in the original concerns the thousandth or several thousandth generation in the second mention fully as much as it concerns the third or fourth generation in the first statement, and unless this be clearly admitted the doctrine of the Decalogue respecting the limited perpetuity of evil and the everlasting duration of righteousness is not brought out, but is beclouded.

The word "jealous," which is often a cause of contention among scholars, can be better rendered "zealous" without doing the slightest violence to the Hebrew text. It surely needs but a slight or superficial study of the incessant outworking of universal law or order, to discover that evil is its own destroyer through the sequence of cause and effect.

The old saying, "Give a murderer rope enough and he will hang himself," was meant to illustrate the obvious fact that sin is its own punishment, or to speak more accurately, its own destroyer Some evils commit suicide; others murder one another, and others again raise up offspring to destroy them. Disorder cannot be of everlasting continuance in this world or in any other sphere or condition of existence as it is opposed to the trend of universal energy. Epes Sargent, in a beautiful hymn found in several Universalist collections, has given the following truly scientific interpretation of the much-disputed passage *"The soul that sinneth it shall surely die,"* by adding to the text this line: *"Die to the sin that did its life confine"*

In some sense all deep thinkers are Universalists, that is, they all agree that error is not immortal for good alone is eternal; and strange though it may sound, this doctrine is quite compatible with the original version of the theological dogma of the everlasting happiness of the righteous and the equally everlasting misery of the wicked

We submit the following propositions inviting all to weigh them carefully and see if they are not reasonable, logical and just:

(1) Righteous living induces the result of blessedness, commonly called the reward of happiness, righteousness being the cause of which happiness is the effect Herein lies the foundation of the doctrine of Heaven.

(2) Unrighteous living induces the result of cursedness commonly called punishment of sin, unright-

eousness being the cause of which misery is the effect. Herein lies the foundation of the doctrine of Hell.

(3) Happiness is coeval with righteousness, misery is likewise coeval with unrighteousness; therefore the relation between the two is in both cases an eternal relation, a relation fixed and unalterable, founded in the Will of God or the Nature of Things.

(4) Unrighteousness is not inherent in the nature of the Universe, and is, therefore, not necessary; but it may be expressed as discord, disorder, disease or abnormality, all of which terms imply vincible conditions, but do not refer to the nature of absolute life which is alone invincible.

(5) As finite entities are capable of making mistakes while engaged in experimental efforts to perfectly manipulate the plastic substances which are given to them in the outworking of divine order to control, the inevitable consequences of wrong doing being painful, and in every way disagreeable, God has so safeguarded the universe from the possibility of falling at any point into hopeless depravity, that the penalties which follow trespass or transgression are necessarily remedial.

No chastening, says a New Testament writer, is momentarily other than distressful, but it yields the peaceable fruits of righteousness in those who are chastised. We confess ourselves thoroughly disgruntled with all controversy for controversy's sake, and we would never lift a finger to gain a wordy victory over a verbal opponent in the course of a debate, but though our motive is utterly pacific, our sole desire being to show the most excellent way of universal harmony, we cannot cry peace, peace, where there is no peace, and tell people complacently that there is no essential distinction between right and wrong, or that it makes no difference whether we live virtuously or viciously.

Candidly speaking, the old orthodox theology with its grim doctrine of capricious foreordination and particular predestination, has left no room for ethics in theology, while the importation of the adjective *vicarious* into all discussions regarding atonement, has thrown many a cloud of dust in the mental eyes of disputants on both sides during utterly needless religious controversies.

The moral law is intended to promote virtue, to suppress vice, to turn the erring into the right path through appeals to love and fear alike. Needless to argue, if we are addressing audiences imbued with the spirit of the higher education, that it is better far to rule by love than fear. It certainly is immeasurably better to appeal to innate love of goodness than to threaten wrongdoers with the awful consequence of guilt. Still, it can never be wrong to employ any method of teaching which strictly accords with truth, and it is quite as true to declare that error produces suffering as to proclaim the sweet beautiful certainty that virtue brings delight to all who practice it.

The Bible is a collection of books presenting a very great many aspects of truth. It is a literature calling for careful study, not a story to be read through as one reads a novel, and for this reason it seems impossible, within anything like reasonable limits of space, to present all the many aspects of truth which are presented in so compendious a collection of writings.

It is sometimes said that the Decalogue and the Beatitudes are the same in essence, but antithetical in form, and it is also said that the Sermon on the Mount and all that follows it in the record of the life and teachings of Jesus is a reverse statement to the teachings of the Hebrew Pentateuch.

The latter is not in our judgment a substantiable criticism, because there are blessings and curses in the Old and New Testaments alike, though in proportion to space occupied the benedictory form of teaching is more conspicuous over the maledictory in the four Gospels than in the five books of the Law. We are not insinuating that readers as a whole are unfamiliar with Leviticus, which has been often called the "Book of Blood," (somewhat unwarrantably unless blood be given a spiritual interpretation) but we have often met with fairly educated people who have been greatly surprised when they heard the following texts quoted from the nineteenth chapter of Leviticus: "Thou shalt not hate thy brother in thy heart—but thou shalt love thy neighbor as thyself," (verses 17-18) And, "The stranger that dwelleth with you shall be unto you as one born among you, and thou shalt love him as thyself," (verse 34.)

Though we are thoroughly in sympathy with every reasonable endeavor to discard all harsh and cruel measures which tyrants seek to justify by quoting Bible passages in their support, we cannot be so servile to vituperative assaults upon the Pentateuch as to remain silent when we hear it flagrantly asserted that the Jewish God is a monster of cruelty, and that we must turn our backs upon the Torah utterly if we are to make progress in the ways of peace and kindliness

If the nineteenth chapter of Leviticus, which contains a re-statement of the Decalogue with many additional commands, should be taken as a guide to life by all people today, there would henceforward be no more ill-will or strife among nations or tale-bearing to the detriment of small communities.

It is constantly the case that, mingled with many grand and noble precepts, there are intermingled some of doubtful significance and apparently of little or no modern importance, therefore the Ten Words from Sinai may be truly regarded as an all-sufficient condensation of Divine Law incumbent upon all humanity.

Concerning the ever fruitful topic of heredity, it requires to be said that a careful reading of the Second Commandment refutes entirely the pessimistic view. taken by multitudes viz., that if we are born heirs to certain distempers, the fathers having eaten "sour grapes" the children's teeth are irretrievably "on edge."

Those who hate God, or in other words those who wilfully or deliberately continue in the accursed state into which some have been born, these, but these only, are involved in the iniquitous generation, a word used again and again in the Bible in a very much wider sense than its commonly obvious meaning.

Consider the following illustration of biblical style and usage: "This is the generation of them that seek Thee, even of them that seek Thy face O God of Israel."

The twenty-fourth Psalm is a beautiful and triumphant canticle of praise in which all the righteous are spoken of as a holy generation regardless of the time and place of their existence. It is highly necessary to take the subject of heredity far out into wider fields than the narrow confines in which it is too often held enclosed, and let it be said frankly and once for all, that if we regard ourselves as bondservants of external conditions, all attempts at moral culture are vain and — every endeavor to change for the better an adverse inherited condition must be entirely unavailing.

It is useless to seek to reconcile blind fatalistic submission to hereditary predispositions with the noble philanthropic efforts now being everywhere made to rescue sufferers from the toils of a depressing environment. The facts of hereditary predisposition or tendency must be dealt with in the proper place from the standpoint of efficient specialists with the logical results of whose discoveries we have no dispute, but the practical educator is surely called upon to show the way out of bondage while many alienists of the materialistic school have only shown the way into captivity.

That there has been a way into a condition in which we now find ourselves, we must of course rest assured and it may be well to unearth that way, so as to warn the present race of men and women liable to become parents, to avoid conducting the unborn into any such inharmonious environment; but the great question before us is, where and what is the way out?

The way in is hatred of God (love of error) according to the Decalogue. The way out is love of God (love of righteousness) according to the same authority. Now, if you are in a pit you wish to be helped out, and if you are at all philanthropic you are not simply satisfied with the negative good of not forcing others in, but you wish to be helpful in assisting out some of your neighbors who are already engulfed.

How should we set to work to overcome hereditary evils? This is now our pertinent enquiry. Theosophists have much to say concerning Karma, and very foggy are some statements and very depressing also, in many instances, because they fancy that Karma is a mysterious something carried over from one incarnation of the soul to another, instead of comprehending it as a continually active force identifiable with the ever-operating law of sequence.

True it undoubtedly is, that "As a man sows so must he reap," but it is not only arbitrary but irrational to build up a hypothesis concerning sowing and reaping which is entirely foreign to the original conception of the Karmic law as declared by the wisest philosophers of the East, whose metaphysical system is not always easily interpreted by Western students.

During July, 1899, a large number of contributors to the Correspondence columns of the *Philadelphia Bulletin* expressed their, for the most part, hazy views on the vexed problems of predestination and free agency, and it was indeed interesting to note how infrequent were any letters which threw any helpful or encouraging light on the infinite question of fore-ordination, or predetermination, which seems no more settled today than when Wesley and his contemporaries threshed the subject out with tireless industry along the old lines of Arminian vs. Calvinistic Theology.

We all know that in most modern pulpits the old Calvinism is practically dead; very few Presbyterians preach it as of yore, but in these days when so-called scientific agnosticism is greatly to the fore, we are far more likely to be carried away with a seemingly scientific substitute than to be led into the trammels of that detestable phase of old theology which wrung from Whittier the telling lines,

"Nothing can be good in Him,
Which evil is in me."

Our real danger today lies in our liability to accept a doctrine of fatalism, largely if not wholly pessimistic, which makes every one of us mere creatures of environment; a doctrine which contains nothing of hope or helpfulness or inspiration to courageous action.

If we are satisfied to be mere lotus-eaters, content to live the life of a poet's indolent Cuthay, we may be resigned to a fatalistic view of life, but such a view comports not at all with the enterprising Western spirit, which needs to be married to Oriental restfulness before a balance can be struck and equilibrium in philosophy be attained. We certainly inherit shapes or moulds into which we are born; our psychical as well as our physical bodies seem to partake of the distinctive qualities including all the peculiarities of our immediate progenitors, and sometimes of quite remote ancestors, if the theory of atavism be demonstratable.

Ibsen, in one of his rather gruesome dramas, has given us an exaggerated view of hereditary compulsion, and like all other fatalists he has sunk into pessimism in company with Max Nordau and many other brilliant intellects who, though keen and analytical to a certain depth, are by no means profound enough to find the indomitable soul, the true ego, which lies behind that exterior mind which is all that these philosophers appear to have discovered.

Very great good is being done by practical "Suggestionists" in the contributions they are making to a distinctive type of psychologic literature. Their highest services are invariably rendered to the cause of human liberty and progress when they discover that in every case the sub-self or "subjective mind" is good in itself and amenable to good suggestions always.

Even among avowedly metaphysical writers we find some ambiguity on the score of relative good and evil, as in nowise incompatible with absolute good only.

Were there such a thing as a bad atom somewhere in the universe, which chanced to get itself incorporated into the fibre of an immortal soul, then we should be confronted with a real problem of evil, and our only lawful inference would be that unless that atom could be destroyed evil must remain a part of the enduring creation. But evils are only discords and discords are all resolvable into harmonies.

We contain nothing in our natures which is essentially or intrinsically other than perfectly good; such was the lesson learned by Peter in his vision of the net let down from Heaven containing all manner of living creatures, some of which he had been accustomed to regard as good and others as evil, (Vide Acts x).

It would be absurd to say that all manners of living creatures, including reptiles and insects as well as birds and quadrupeds, stand for individual human beings in the sense that one man for example is all vulture and another all dove; but it is true that the elements or ingredients which go to form all creatures collectively have their place in the collective and also in the individual human economy.

It is only as we realize the "child of God" or higher self, which is the abiding self of every one of us, that we can see our way to conquest over the "child of man" which is not evil but rightly is subordinate. When we come to realize that all things are ours to subdue, we render obedience to the highest and exact submission from the lowest, thereby bringing order out of chaos without altering the essential nature of a single atom contained in that chaos which we are resolving into cosmos.

If we are in the generation of the unrighteous, if we "sit in the seat of the scornful," if we live according to the way of those who have no "fear of God before their eyes," then are we subject unto the operation of law on the side of penalty; but if we arise out of that lower state and betake ourselves to the mountain tops of virtuous living, the same immutable law works for us on the side of benediction.

A mountain climber may be under a cloud when it bursts so that the rain must fall down upon him, but if he be above that cloud the rain still falls into the valley beneath, but it is clear sky over his head. The law is no respecter of persons, but it is a perfect respecter of situations. If you do not get wet it is because you are above the cloud, not because you are singled out as a special object of the cloud's approval.

A partial Deity is an idol; the only God intelligent humanity can reverence is the God of nature, who is also God of grace to all who have found the way to live above their lower nature in the enjoyment of the privileges accruing, not from place of birth or creed or parentage, but from the ascension of the individual above the plane where the law operates as people vainly think unmercifully.

The penalties which follow upon evil-doing are just as good in their own day, and considering the purposes they have to serve, as are the enjoyments which follow upon the noblest conduct; therefore, harsh though it may seem to say it, there is no cruelty in the idea couched in the startling statement "God can be just as happy in contemplating the unhappiness, as in viewing the happiness of His children."

Such a statement is indefensible if those who make it believe that suffering is anything other than educational. Our grief is due to our shortsightedness, and even Robert Ingersoll, agnostic though he was, said this very thing in substance in many of his lectures. Though we could never agree with all the witty Colonel's sarcasm and diatribe, we found much to admire in Ingersoll's soberest and kindliest sayings, and now that he has quitted the scene of his mortal experiences, we may well look back upon his singular career, to prize the good things he said and remember his many kindly actions while oblivion may embrace the limitations of his view when he strove to scan a spiritual horizon.

Everything earthly is but relative, and we must know to what this relative is related in the wider circle of human experience before we are justified in crying out against any divine or natural dispensation. The sickness and sorrows we bemoan are legitimate fruits of the seeds we have been ignorantly sowing, and as we are certainly here on earth to develop self-conscious individuality by actual contact with the universal negative to which we give the conventional name of matter, all our bitter experiences are due to our own mistakes, and their bitterness is necessary for a season so that we shall not remain satisfied with any erroneous or imperfect statements or conclusions.

Good alone is eternal; blessedness alone is endless; all suffering is temporal and disciplinary! Such is the message of the Second Commandment!

LECTURE FOUR.

THE THIRD COMMANDMENT.

"Thou shalt not take the name of the Lord thy God in vain."

As we proceed with our expositions of the Ten Commandments, we find that the well-known texts are capable of suggesting vastly more than an obvious and conventional elucidation of their language.

It is only when we allow ourselves to float away, so to speak, on the current of a great suggestion, that we lose sight of the local incidences of the matter in hand, and find that we are transported into a realm of life and action absolutely unbounded by special time or place.

So-called "higher criticisms" are often practically valueless to ninety-nine people out of every hundred though they have a distinctive value for professors and students in seats of learning. What we all need most is not a learned account of when, where and how certain choice fragments of doctrine were brought together, but hints and helps toward beautifying and glorifying our own immediate times and circumstances.

Profane language is always to be condemned, and whenever it is accounted vulgar in polite circles, many resonant voices are raised against it. But the Third Commandment, though it unmistakably declares that none are held guiltless who take the name of God in vain, it has by no means exhausted its admonitions when we reverently accept it as a powerful remonstrant against levity in speech, in cases where the Divine Name or any of its equivalents are idly spoken.

The word "name," on which so much hinges in this commandment, means immeasurably more than a superficial reading can suggest. Names were always originally indicative of the character, and often of the occupation of those who bore them. If any one will take time to consult a dictionary of Bible names, and then read a chapter from any one of the books of the Bible, substituting the translated name for the original, the narrative, whatever it may be, will be instantly brought up to date; all its archaisms will have vanished, and we shall feel ourselves standing in the presence of a modern picture and listening to words of revelation spoken in our own familiar tongue.

Moses means one who has been drawn out of water. Aaron signifies one who is lofty and intellectually enlightened. Moses is he who has risen above the intellectual (watery) plane of human consciousness, and has been illumined by the divine fire of inmost love and wisdom.

We read everywhere concerning Moses of the behavior of the intuitive, and in connection with Aaron of the conduct of the simply intellectual type of humanity, and we cannot fail to discern how easy it was for the people to compel Aaron to minister to their love of idols, while Moses brake in pieces the calf of gold, which his brother had fashioned at the people's request, immediately he returned into the camp from the mountain summit.

Intuitive perception of truth leads where unaided intellect can only follow. Moses and Aaron are brothers, and Aaron is always the elder of the two because intellectual development precedes spiritual illumination in the orderly process of human regeneration. The new and higher birth of the embodied soul into celestial consciousness adds to its possessions of knowledge, but never removes information intellectually received.

As we advance higher and penetrate more deeply into the universal arcana, we cannot give up or forfeit any of our former possessions while we are perpetually adding to our conscious store. Moses knows more than Aaron; the younger must rule the people in preference to the elder, for that which is latest born is highest born, and to this truth the scientific doctrine of evolution abundantly testifies.

The Ten Commandments may be compared to a ladder. The foundation is uncompromising monotheism, "Have we not all one Father, hath not one God created us all?" Theology and theocracy are so inextricably interwoven with anthropology and democracy, that they are virtually inseparable. It is a most welcome reflection which follows naturally upon a perusal of agnostic and even of avowedly infidel literature, that the chief attacks upon ideas of Deity commonly entertained in the religious world are leveled against conceptions of God which are, at root, so odious that we can fearlessly assert that it would be better to entertain no God-idea at all than entertain so hideous a travesty.

Name means character; therefore, "Thou shalt not take the name of the Lord thy God in vain," means, primarily, thou shalt not attribute to the Supreme Being attributes and actions which thou wouldst scorn with indignation, were they attributed to thee.

What is called "liberal religion," or "new progressive orthodoxy" in Christian circles today, is only a clarified and amplified statement of views expressed by enlightened thinkers everywhere and through all ages. Much that is styled new today is extremely old, and nowhere is this rendered more evident than in many treatises upon the "new" woman, whose portrait was painted by Solomon, or Lemuel or whoever wrote the thirty-first chapter of Proverbs many a century before what is now termed "Woman Suffrage," or "Political Equality" called for advocacy among the nations of the West.

That is a narrow view taken by many commentators, who say that the God of the Old Testament is not the God of the New Testament, because the common ideas of God entertained by ancient Jews were vastly inferior to those proclaimed by Jesus.

Marie Corelli, in one of her short stories, "The Song of Miriam," and also in her exceedingly forceful book, "Barabbas," has unduly dwelt upon the harsher aspects of the Old Testament conception of Deity. Henry Wood, in "Victor Sirenus," has fallen into the same error. It seems very difficult indeed for any writer who is earnest and enthusiastic and fired with strong convictions, to altogether escape prejudice and to steer entirely clear of bias, when alluding to the peoples and products of other lands and ages than those with which the author feels most vitally in sympathy. It is equally the case when sympathies are very strongly aroused in any direction, for then as much too much is said in favor of the favored side as is said in opposition to the side disfavored.

There is really no conflict between the essence of Judaism and the spirit of Christianity. The letter of the two systems is certainly at variance, but the soul of both is the same. When in the model prayer of the Gospels we find the clause "Hallowed be thy Name," we are at once taken back to the Decalogue and reminded of the third command from Sinai. Thou shalt hallow the divine name, is the spiritual rendering; whenever people are ready for spiritual interpretations it is time to let go of all further clinging to the negative form of the same commandment.

To look at a subject on both sides is to treat that subject with judicial fairness; then if we find one side far more beautiful than the other, we are doing quite right to expose the loveliest side to public view. It has been unwisely said that it is easier to obey a negative than an affirmative command. This is certainly not invariably the case, and as this aspect of the situation is of great importance to parents and teachers everywhere, we beg to insist that very many of the severest hardships encountered by guardians and directors of the young grow out of the erroneous use of the unpleasant formula "thou shalt not," to the almost total exclusion of the delightful and encouraging phrase "thou shalt."

Thou shalt pronounce the divine name with reverence. Herein lies the gist of the Third Commandment. The strictly orthodox Jew, who is a rigid literalist, deems it necessary to bring a scroll of the Law into a court room and to swear with his hand upon the sacred parchment. Many Christians deem it necessary to kiss a Bible so that they may be bound by their oath, but Quakers who will only affirm, as they take literally the words of the Sermon on the Mount: "Swear not at all," are found quite as reliable after their simple affirmation as people of other creeds who have kissed books or sworn with their hands on parchment.

Doubtless a primitive or undisciplined state of feeling demands an impressive ritual. "So help me God," is a phrase which grates harshly on many sensitive ears, though it greatly helps some people who need an external or verbal stimulant to enable them to keep their word. Such an expression does not imply taking the name of God in vain, unless one uses the expression with intent to deceive or cheat a neighbor or else so thoughtlessly that it leaves no impression on the memory even of the one who has pronounced it. Such an ejaculation may be sometimes a prayer, a sincere aspiration for divine help and guidance, and when it is thus honest and fervent, even though some scientists will class it with simple auto-suggestions, it will assuredly bear satisfactory fruit. Developed natures have absolutely no need for it.

When you say that a man's word is his bond, you imply that it would be altogether superfluous to bond him otherwise. "According to thy word it shall be unto thee," and "According to thy word be it unto thee," are two declarations covering the entire subject of oaths and affirmations. Take the first of these sentences and regard it as a prophecy of universal import. See how it illuminates the books of the Law. "An eye for an eye, and a tooth for a tooth" is everlasting justice which none can escape, for the time will never come when we can knock out our neighbor's teeth or pluck out our neighbor's eyes and not incur a penalty.

People love to sing, "Free from the law, oh, happy condition," but unless they are very cautious in their interpretation of what they sing, they are apt to degenerate into utter lawlessness, then they need to be told again that license is not liberty and freedom is secured by righteous law.

Let us be solemnly ethical in our theology; we may surpass simple morality but we must never fall below it. The great vice of Calvinism consists in its pernicious dogma of misconceived election. "The King can do no wrong," shouts the idolatrous monarchist. "The elect can do no wrong," screams the upholder of the doctrine of preterition.

Antinomians, who were very plentiful a century or more ago, declared openly that God's elect people could not possibly do any evil in the sight of Heaven, no matter what crimes they might be guilty of, and they also taught with equal vociferation that the non-elect could do naught that was other than displeasing to the Almighty, no matter how sweet and virtuous their lives among men might prove.

Contrast this abominable heresy with such fine Jewish teaching as "God's people are all the righteous ones," and Paul's declaration that whoever worketh righteousness is acceptable to the All-righteous One. The practical ethical culturist or moral educator will not hesitate an instant between Judaism and Calvinism, if the choice be offered him.

"The Lord will hold no one guiltless who swears falsely," said the ancient prophet "Show me thy faith by thy works," said James the Apostle, to those in his day who taught that belief, not character, was of supremest moment. Beliefs are largely influenced by circumstances, by place of birth, by early training, by the associations of later years, and by a thousand features of environment which have absolutely nothing to do with good will or noble character; but fidelity or infidelity to a trust, compliance or non-compliance with the terms of a voluntary self-signed contract, the resolve to keep or break one's word, these and all kindred considerations have to do with the very fundamentals of ethics, and cannot be lightly esteemed by any who are seeking to impress upon the growing generation the need of strict integrity in thought, word and deed, as the supreme passport to happiness on earth and blessedness in Heaven.

Among the many objectionable practices in which people often indulge, and which are certainly rebuked in the Third Commandment, is that of calling upon God in the most shocking way to do something dreadful to us if we do not do certain things ourselves. The intention of the speaker in such a case is to impress the bystanders, without usually much, if any, deep thought of the dreadful import of the spoken word; but we have clearly no right to call upon God to visit us with calamities, as the very act itself is one of presumption and of blasphemy.

Treating the subject from the standpoint of Occultism, it is easy enough to see what was intended by the old proverb, "Curses, like chickens, always come home to roost." Substitute the word "blessings," and you can enforce the lesson of the proverb in a far gentler and pleasanter, but in none the less forcible a way. The simple fact of echo serves to illustrate one of the profoundest truths taught by the world's greatest seers and sages, viz., the certainty with which psychic utterances return upon the sender.

No one can possibly go out among resounding rocks and hills and utter words of good and wise intent, without the answering echo giving back the identical words sent forth. In like manner the same reverberating rocks and hills must reply with maledictions to those who contaminate the air with foul or cruel speech.

We may never be fully certain of the extent of influence we can exert on others. Mental treatments may easily enough be given, but we cannot be assured that in every instance they will be received or taken by those to whom they are intentionally sent. The effect upon ourselves in every case is indubitable, because of the kind and rate of vibration we set up by speaking, or even by quietly thinking, in our own organisms.

To bless is to be blessed. He who blesses others blesses himself as well; and he who seeks or wills to bless another, whether that other is open to receive the proffered boon or not, blesses himself by uttering any word of heartfelt benediction, no matter toward whom the good wish is projected. We are never sympathetic with unduly harsh interpretations of scripture, nor do we believe that harsh renderings are true; but it is simply namby-pambyism to gloss over all the sterner aspects of a moral revelation and feed the Children of Israel, or any other children. on an innutritious diet of sweetmeats only. Bitter herbs are necessary factors in the Passover meal, and many of the precepts of the Law, though sweet as honey in the inward parts, after they have been assimilated and digested, are very bitter in their first taste when they begin to enter the mouth of understanding.

It seems to be the opinion of many would-be teachers of the young in these days, that every moral pill should be disguised and sugar-coated so that children should be led to swallow medicine unawares. With such a policy we do not agree, because it often results in distrust and moral nausea. Many children have been injured rather than aided by medicines clandestinely administered in jam or coffee. If it is necessary to take a bitter dose, let's take it manfully; bitters and acids are just as good as sweets in their own day and generation, as they have a work of beneficence to accomplish which sweets are powerless to perform.

Penalties due to transgression are meted out by the same wise loving Providence which rewards our virtuous actions, therefore, we must be quite as thankful for the blow that smites as for the balm that heals. This may be a difficult doctrine to accept without reflection, but it is the only sound and reasonable consolation for the afflicted.

We cannot make intelligent people believe they are not in pain when they are suffering agony, but if we are truly wise, we can induce them to look at their afflictions in an entirely new and altogether comforting.

and salutary light. The great unsolved, though not necessarily unsolvable problem of the ages, is why are we called upon to suffer? Suffering is incidental to growth in an experimental world provided we make the mistakes which occasion it, but not otherwise.

Colonel Robert G. Ingersoll was called a blasphemer times without number, but among the characteristic sayings of Ingersoll occurs the following: "I would like to see this world without crime and without a tear." Such a sentiment is in itself truly beautiful and reflects credit upon whoever entertains it, but it is possible that a good-hearted man, like the famed agnostic lecturer and lawyer, may not have clearly seen how to rid the world of crimes and tears. To inveigh against a malady is not to remedy it, for remedies are to be found only in conquest, not in complaint. We may bemoan iniquities and weep over the sorrows of those about us, thereby evincing genuine kindheartedness, without being able (through lack of insight into causes) to overcome a single one of the evils we desire to see removed.

People too often forget that we are here to develop individual characters, and that law must be inexorable to render possible our development. It is from shortsightedness on the part of many writers on both sides of a controversy that so-called metaphysical literature is heavily weighted with rash denials and affirmations. Writers against metaphysical healing are never tired of exposing the absurdity of denying the present temporary existence of ailments which mental practitioners are often paid to cure.

If by reason of "taking the name of God in vain," we are suffering the penalty of this irreverence, it is useless to deny the existence of the legal penalty or plead guiltless when we are convicted of error.

The proper attitude to take when we are suffering the consequence of folly, is to look our penalty in the face and accept it thankfully, a course which would truly be impossible if we did not discern something of the beneficial object for which the penalty is administered.

While dealing with the question of penalty, let us look to our own ways in this concern. A child has committed some offense, and in order to bring home to him 'a truth he needs to become familiar with, a wise teacher or parent gives him a lesson to learn or some useful task to perform. Such a task can never resemble walking the treadmill or picking oakum, nor should it ever be any sort of useless occupation, but invariably a work use-

ful in itself as to its results, and particularly
adapted to counteract the special vice which it is meant
to conquer.

Mere punishments only harden. Men and women
grow callous in prisons and soon attain a sullen indif-
ference to a life of degradation which is the very reverse
of beneficial in its reactionary influence upon society at
large. All penalties must be educational to be
righteous, and when they are such, prison reform will
no longer be the difficult measure it has long been
found to be.

The Lord never punishes as man punishes. Those
who attribute to God baseness and pettiness resembling
their own mistaken motives of right government, would
do well to note the deep significance of the immortal
saying, "Love is the fulfilling of the Law." So long as
there are quibbles concerning justice as opposed to
mercy, it is plain that the meaning of equity has not
been found.

Charity is a sweet word, and when it is rendered as
the alternate of love, there is none grander in the entire
lexicon; but so long as justice is forgotten and
so-called but unreal charity is extolled at the expense
of equitable dealing, there must be riots and insurrec-
tions and manifold outcries against laws that are,
truly speaking, illegal and against miscalled order
which is but disorder in disguise.

Much that is called Anarchy is not an intentional
protest against law and order on the part of outraged
famishing multitudes, who in their desperation resort
to frantic violence to redress their wrongs. The cry
of all such is for justice against injustice, and if they
declare themselves lawless it is because the only law
they have known has been a law of oppression and
cruelty.

Edna Lyall, one of the most religious of popular
novelists, has not hesitated in "We Two," and others
of her noble books, to handle the "blasphemy laws"
without restraint. One of her leading characters
strongly resembles Charles Bradlaugh in many telling
features, and she no doubt got much material for "We
Two" (a pathetic story of a devoted father and
daughter) from the celebrated discussions which at one
time literally convulsed the thought of England on the
question whether a "blasphemer" might sit in the House
of Commons, after he had been elected member for
Northampton by an overwhelming majority of qualified
rate-payers.

Agnostics can never be fairly accused of blasphemy,
but Bradlaugh openly proclaimed himself an atheist;

but honest atheists are not blasphemers for as they deny that any Deity exists it is impossible that they should speak wilfully against the Being whose very existence they deny. Atheism may be blindness and stultification, but it is not blasphemy He who knows nothing of God and frankly declares that the name of the Supreme Being conveys no image to his mind, is not in any sense one who takes the name of God in vain; but they who make free with the name of the Almighty and accuse God of crimes against love and justice, which they themselves would not commit, are the real blasphemers.

On Sunday, July 23, 1899, many a pulpit rang with the truthful declaration that Ingersoll's infidelity was largely induced by the lovelessness of the theology forced upon him in his childhood, and by the very sour and often grossly hypocritical lives of loudly professing religionists.

As name and nature mean the same, they who take God's name in vain are they who sin against the divine attributes, whether they embody them in their thought in a divine Person or not. Do you love righteousness? Do you love love? Do you love truth? Do you love justice and mercy combined in equity If you do you love God, whether you have or have not an intellectual conception of God in your creed or declaration of opinions.

In the New Testament there is much said about "The name which is above every name," and "the name whereby we must be saved."

If we ask in the name of Jesus it is in the spirit which is manifested through the Uplifter of the race. If you are in the love of things divine, you must be saved; to be in the love of truth and goodness is to be in the only affection that can truly save. People are not safe for heaven because they are professing Christians, nor in danger of condemnation because they are outside the nominally Christian fold. It is but a trick of priestcraft to exalt sacraments, extol ordinances and glorify shibboleth so that the path to heaven appears a road of diction and ceremony instead of a pathway of loving kindness.

Who can say that the creedful man is any nobler than his creedless brother? Who can prove that churchgoers are any truer than their non-church going neighbors? Man looks ever at some outward appearance, while God views the heart No one is ever safer than his inmost affection makes him; none are higher in spiritual life than their deepest love has carried them. Away with all the cant and illusion of empty profession, for it is the pretense of a cloud which contains no water wherewith to refresh the thirsty earth.

Missionary enterprises are largely farcical; contributions to missionary endeavor are steadily decreasing, for the "heathen" are finding "Christians" out. Will you neglect want at your own door that you may irritate the placid Hindu with an invitation to an English church and roast mutton, when in his own way he is quite as near to Para-Brahm as you may be to Adonai or to Jesus.

All people cannot pray or praise in the same tongue. "Some call it evolution and others call it God" is a poet's way of saying that seekers after truth are everywhere endeavoring to interpret the phenomena of Nature upon which they reverently gaze, each in his own way; and, we who say it is God working in, through, and by evolution, have no dispute with any who are seeking and groping after a truth so infinite that no intellect can grasp it in its perfection.

There is nothing of sweetness and light in the impudence of bigotry which is altogether sour and dark. Those priests who repeat like parrots the untranslated phrase, "there is no salvation outside the one holy universal church," are dealing treacherously with the people if they insinuate that that church is Roman, Greek, Anglican, Evangelical, or aught else that is sectional.

No one is saved until he enters the true living universal church of the Holy Spirit, which embraces the pure, upright, merciful, and loving of all climes and nations. For such is "the church of the first-born whose names are written in Heaven." The mighty thunderings of Divine Law are terrors to evil-doers, that such may cease to do evil and learn to do well; but they are misinterpreted if any one of them is taken to mean aught other than the pleadings of divine beneficence. No drunkard, thief, adulterer, nor covetous person enters the kingdom of Heaven; therefore, that all may enter it at last, there must be what men call hells and purgatories, houses of correction, states (if not places) of corrective chastisement in this world, and wherever else in the universe such may be required. Verily the worm shall not die so long as there is filth for it to devour at the mouth of Gehenna, and verily the flame shall not be quenched until every particle of error and every vestige of uncleanness has been consumed in its purifying blaze.

Sinai is in the wilderness; Zion is in the promised land. While we are in the wilderness we are within sight and sound of Sinai, and as Shakespeare has truly told us in the immortal soliloquy of "Hamlet," "Conscience doth make cowards of us all." But heart of grace, ye travelers; you shall all reach Canaan, and then that same conscience shall make heroes of you all. The Lord will never hold you guiltless so long as you take his name in vain, but you will not always profane your sanctuary, you will not always defile your temple; you will all come some day under the spell of the anthem "Blessed are all they who love the Law and delight to observe its precepts." The common practice of using profane language is with many people little more than a bad habit, picked up on the street. Such a habit is an offense against decency, and should be promptly put down, but it is not-intentional blasphemy. Mere careless flippancy of the tongue is not sin in the heart; it would be cruel and unjust to tell the vulgar user of fashionable bad language that he is a sinner in the sight of Heaven, when he is only a simpleton who imagines that it is manly and "the correct thing" to echo the vulgarity of fashionable clubs and aristocratic boarding schools.

It is a far more serious matter to trifle with one's word, and it is an awful thing to call God to witness to a lie. Caution and discretion are ever necessary to genuine valor; no one is a coward because he is duly cautious. To think before speaking and to look before leaping is ever the course of the valiant man; but when a pledge has been signed and a word given, though you have sworn to your own hindrance, your word holds you. It is then too late to draw back.

How marvelously God is revealed in the postoffice system of all civilized countries today. You have posted your letter and you cannot withdraw it from the box or bag. God is again revealed in the Sinai of our telegraphic system, and in the profound mysteries of the submarine cable. You have sent your message and you cannot recall it. No matter how many letters, telegrams or cablegrams you may send afterward, you cannot take back the words which you have already committed to the charge of God's omnipresent servant, electricity. God is in today's lightning and nowhere more prominently revealed than in that very force you chain to do your bidding, and which serves you humbly, but magnificently on God's terms, and on no others.

If the agnostic fails to find God in Nature, he discovers at least a law that is immutable. If Deity is not found by the honest sceptic, order which is changeless is discovered by every scientist, no matter where he interrogates the universe.

Ingersoll, agnostic though he was, paid many mighty and eloquent tributes to the Unknown God (who seemed to him to be unknowable) when he voiced the Gospel in his own creed, and paid tribute as a lawyer to the inflexibility of the Law of Nature. The Gospel is in the Law; it is the soul of it. Zion is the heart of Sinai; the Sermon on the Mount is first the Sermon in the Mount. There shall ever be exacted one eye and one tooth in return for the same, and so long as man sheds his brother's blood, that blood will cry for vengeance upon him from the ground which has absorbed it. None are held guiltless who have opposed themselves to irreversible order.

What folly it is to talk of breaking the law. There never were any law-breakers, and there never can be any, but all who oppose the law are opposed success-fully by it; it is they, not the law, who must needs be broken.

It cannot now be long before the many discording voices which agitate the enquiring world will melt into a grand new harmony, such as was necessarily impos-sible in olden days, when lack of that knowledge of each other, which is only born of free social inter-course, made differences seem disagreements. We cannot agree to disagree, but we must agree to differ. The five great races into which the human family is divided may remain as distinct as the five fingers of the human hand, all growing out of one palm, and all essential to the integrity of the total member.

"Thou shalt not take the name of the Lord thy God in vain" is as much a message to the Brahmin and to the Buddhist, as it is to the Jew and to the Christian. God never leaves himself without witness in human conscience. Dr. James Martineau, one of the most venerable and intuitive of the religious writers of the Nineteenth century, has rendered glorious service to the cause of universal religion even in his most critical works with which some of his friends may not be able to wholly sympathize. In his masterly volume, "The Seat of Authority in Religion," Dr. Martineau has shown that even though there be no reasonable ground for accepting ecclesiastical or sacerdotal authority of any sort, the teaching of one of his own magnificent hymns will prove all the truer for humanity.

"He who himself and God would know,
Into the silence let him go,
And, lifting off pall after pall
Reach to the inmost depth of all!"

What matters any geographical or chronological aspect of Sinai? What matters the authenticity of the Mosaic Pentateuch from the standpoint of Colenso and the later critics? "Thou shalt not take the name of the Lord thy God in vain," is today's message from the seat of authoritative revelation within, and woe betide whoever proves false to the voice of the spirit within him.

What signifies verbal orthodoxy or heterodoxy; orthodoxy is your doxy whoever you may be and whatever you may believe; heterodoxy in your eyes is the sum of opinions on which you have not deigned to set the seal of your personal approval.

We need to listen to Emerson, and to all other great philosophers who have turned from tables of stone without to tables of spirit within. The soul is its own witness. It is, as Emerson said, original and solitary. It is mature in the infant; it speaks with no uncertain tone even in those who are insolently called urchins and street Arabs. If you believe in natural human depravity you outrage the Decalogue, for the law expects no one to perform an impossibility, and Sinai's trumpet call is to every listener to hear and to obey.

Theologians have dared to say that God gives a law which man cannot keep, and that the well-beloved Son must keep it for them as their substitute. Such is not the voice from Sinai, neither is it the symphony of Zion. From the holier mountain the higher heavenly music sounds in dulcet accents "I, being lifted up will draw all humanity unto me," and, "Be ye of good courage, for I have overcome the world."

If the law is to be fulfilled in love, then are we all counselled so to fulfill it. Larger insight follows upon the smaller earlier view. The children of Israel, "babes in Christ" have not yet heard the inner voice nor been able to discern the deeper message. How significant is the veiling of the face of Moses by request of the people; not eagles, but owls, rather, were the members of the congregation which Moses faced when he came down from the mountain and resumed his task of seeking to lead a nomadic multitude out of carnal bondage into spiritual liberty. If today's Moses covers his face it is because you have requested him to do so. If today's revelations to you are obscure, literal and harsh, it is because you are not ready to listen to the voice that speaketh from heaven in deeper and in sweeter melody.

The sign of the prophet Jonah is the only sign which can ever be given to an evil and adulterous generation. The whole book of Jonah is in the Third Commandment. Let us not ridicule as "an old fish story" a poem and a parable, a living allegory, which sets forth for all time the consequences of disobedience to a heavenly vision and analyses to perfection the motives which have led to that disobedience. Let us not laugh at Elisha's baldness, nor scoff at the two she-bears who devour forty-two impertinent children. Laugh if you will at what seems to you to be but comical tales from a credulous past, but take heed lest while sneering at the letter you cast away the spirit which giveth life.

Shallow scoffing at correspondential imagery resolves itself at length into diatribe leveled against nut-shells as an article of diet. We all need spiritual nut-crackers, without them we cannot read any Bible. The kernels within the shells are for our nutriment; when we are eating the delicious meat of the nuts we feel no disposition to revile the shells that once were necessary to preserve it. "To thine own self be true." Shakespeare is a good commentator. Be we all obedient to the inner voice; let us follow the inner light and we shall never walk in darkness.

If we need thunder, we shall hear thunder, but when we are ready for heavenly whisperings we shall hear the still small voice. The Lord is not in the tempest, but the fierce hurricane and the devouring flame make straight the way for the approach of Truth, which always comes to us in proportion as we are able to bear it.

LECTURE FIVE.

THE FOURTH COMMANDMENT.

"Remember that thou keep holy the Sabbath day."

The sentence from the Fourth Commandment quoted above, though frequently put forward as though it constituted the entire command, is really exactly one-seventh of the commandment, which also reads, "Six days shalt thou labor, and do all thy work." Six-sevenths of this commandment relates to what we call work, and one-seventh to what we term rest. Rest and work are so inextricably interwoven in the warp and woof of things, that the great problem to be solved is how to so combine them that we may learn to work restfully and rest actively.

The first chapter of Genesis contains the declaration that God is a Sabbath-keeper, working for six days and then enjoying a period of repose. Needless ridicule has been heaped upon this saying by those whose biblical criticism is confined to the literal text only, and that text they by no means fully understand.

Rest and work are both involved in the world plan, in the universal order. God does not ask us to do what He does not do Himself; this is a fair inference, and this was undoubtedly in the thought of Moses and the other scribes who long before the time of Ezra produced in sections the material out of which the Pentateuch gradually grew.

"Remember" is a word which immediately suggests recollection and reminiscence. The Sabbath law is older than the twentieth chapter of Exodus. Sabbath observances are more ancient by far than the period of the personal Moses who announced to the Israelites in the Arabian wilderness the Law which he declared he did not invent or formulate, but simply made public. A genius is often described as one who thinks God's thoughts after Him. Everyday talent is only imitative, while genius is original and creative, and, though there is nothing new under the sun *per se,* there are many revelations which are new and others which are old to the people to whom those revelations are particularly addressed.

The Decalogue is not by any means a string of novelties or a set of purely original propositions, and as this fact is well known to all who have given it the least historical study, there is nothing startling or revolutionary in such an announcement, even when made by those who put it forward as a reason for shaping the popular faith in the Ten Commandments as a divine revelation.

Divine law makes provision for human nature in its entirety. Body and soul are yokefellows; the care of the one is essential to the welfare of the other. Herein lies the essential truth of metaphysics, which, when completely dissociated from the mass of unprovable assertion with which metaphysical truths are often surrounded, is a gospel of good tidings adapted to every department of human life and activity. The comprehensive inclusiveness of the Sabbath law is clearly seen in its equal application to human beings, to animals, and to the land also.

The narrow Sabbatarian, who makes the holy day the very reverse of a holiday and condemns children to the rigors of a hard, unlovely, puritanical observance from which multitudes have turned away in later years with disgust and anger, is largely responsible for the protest against Sabbath keeping which is now fiercely rampant in many quarters where the non-observance of a weekly rest-day contributes immensely to neurotic disorders of every variety.

If the original Sabbath law had reference to religious exercises only, it could not have been enforced, as it certainly was, with regard to animals who were never required to attend a place of worship or to engage in any exercises of devotion, nor could it have been binding upon the farmer to till the soil for six years, and then let the land rest during the seventh year.

Instead of the reference to God's creation of the world being intended to support a theory of six days of creative work, each of only twenty-four hours duration, the fact that there are six years during which land is to be tilled and the seventh year when it is to lie fallow, shows that such brief days, as we are ordinarily accustomed to reckon, have no necessary connection with the order of creation; but the mystery and meaning of the number seven is obviously alluded to throughout.

Psychology and physiology are completely at one in this teaching. One rest day out of every seven is mentally and physically beneficial to all who take advantage of it; therefore in the interests of the human mind and body we are fully prepared to advocate Sabbath keeping of a rational sort on the platform of any Secular Society, or in any hall of Science in any part of the world.

Religion is not something that stands apart or aloof from all the material interests of humanity, therefore there is very much attention given to dietary rules and to all matters pertaining to cleanliness in the Pentateuch. Those Christians who are particularly anxious to repudiate Judaism, both in letter and in spirit, go to absurd extremes in quoting from the gospels rules and precepts which do not touch the essence of Mosaic legislation at any point as though they bore decidedly against it.

There are always two sides to every subject, the inner and the outer, and the outer can never be of equal importance with the iner. "Clean hands and a pure heart," taken literally, cannot be of equal value; therefore the disciples of Jesus are told by their Master that it is not the soiled condition of physical hands which constitutes the defilement of those who are defiled, but the injustice which they practice in connection with their manual industries. In the esoteric sense of the Law's teaching to be guilty of unclean hands is to employ those members in works of dishonesty or in any deeds of unrighteousness. At the same time physiologists come forward today and tell us that it is essential to health to handle food with literally clean hands, and to be cleanly in all kitchen arrangements, because dirt, microbes and disease are never separable.

The entire Torah is full of legislative enactments which spiritually concern the inmost life of the soul, while outwardly they deal with hygienic provisions for the external side of human comfort and well-being. The Sabbath law is not a dead issue; it is one of the most thoroughly alive questions of today, and instead of its falling into desuetude it is being brought most prominently to the front as a factor in present legislation. Let us see what the Fourth Commandment really counsels in this regard. It says nothing of temple, church or synagogue, and nothing of any devotional rites. In its majestic simplicity it says, "Thou shalt not do any work, neither thou, nor thy son, nor thy daughter, nor thy man-servant, nor thy maid-servant, nor thy cattle nor the stranger that is within thy gates."

Here is strict legislation, to forbid the exaction of an undue amount of labor, either from servants or from animals.. Truth is the word of God; whoever discovers truth speaks God's word after Him. Whatever is most conducive to human welfare is God's will concerning humanity. Laws from heaven are not given to be irksome or unduly restrictive of human freedom; they are revealed as guide posts that we may see our way to the port of health and happiness, for which we are all steering intentionally, however widely we in ignorance may stray from the safe and certain road that leads thereto.

To understand the institution of the Sabbath we need to grasp the import of the words of Jesus, "The Sabbath was made for man, not man for the Sabbath." There were Sabbatarians in Judea, two thousand years or less ago, so extreme in their exaggerated literalism that they actually discussed in grave assemblies the, to us, ludicrous question whether it were lawful to eat an egg on the following day which a hen had laid during the sacred Sabbath.

The New Testament contains a philosophical reply to those extremists who had exalted the Midrash and other empirical commentaries upon the Law far above the text of the Pentateuch itself, therefore, without some knowledge of the Talmud, its contents and origin, the commentator upon much of the New Testament is apt to misconstrue its literal application.

The disciples of Jesus violated a great many rabbinical counsels, among which were many prescriptions with reference to the Sabbath, some of which are in vogue among strictly orthodox Jews at the present moment.

Piles of traditions have so encumbered the original Law that it is often next to impossible to catch glimpses of the purity of the ancient precepts beneath such an immense array of superincumbent ordinances. All great legal instruments are subject to disfigurement in after years, and in no case do we find a more striking instance of subsequent adulterations and falsifications of the spirit of an original, than in the present actual government of the United States of America when we contrast it with those two marvelously compact legal instruments which avowedly constitute the foundation of American administration—the Constitution of the United States and the Declaration of Independence.

Speaking secularly on the Fourth Commandment, we may truly insist that physiology supports the Decalogue. Moses was an anthropologist of the highest rank, a man who knew what was good for the health of a people, even though he had no special divine aid or heaven-born inspiration. A wise leader always insists upon the observance of health rules which are essential to the well-being of the people whom he is seeking to lead out of bondage into liberty, regardless of the particular form of servitude from which he is seeking to deliver them; and as health and morals always go together it is but specious sophistry to seek to separate them. A sufficient code of morals must contain adequate provision for bodily health as well as guidance for spiritual welfare.

The spirit of today, the modern Zeitgeist, is calling loudly for shorter hours of labor, higher wages and more numerous holidays for the people. America is improving greatly in consequence of the attention now being paid to reasonable demands made by the toiling multitudes, that they shall be treated as human beings in the fullest sense of the word, not merely as "factory hands," or automatic pieces of living machinery, to be treated as though they had neither mind nor feeling.

The better treatment of animals, everywhere called for, is another sign of the growing civilization of the times, and it is extremely interesting to note that the humanest measures called for today, are in exact accord with the noblest precepts to be found in ancient books of legislation. No one can toil incessantly week in and week out, without paying the penalty in mental and physical degeneration, and it is surely wretched economy to wear out unnecessarily the machinery essential to the carrying out of the work to which one is devoting one's constant energies. The great blessing of a public rest and recreation day is that it stops the whirr and buzz of machinery, and gives the people *en masse* an opportunity to enjoy their rest together.

We fully support conscientious Jews, Seventh-day Adventists, and all others who insist that they have a right to rest on Saturday and work on Sunday, because they believe that God commanded the seventh, not the first day of the week to be kept holy; but it is certainly desirable in the interest of the nerves of the general public that as much be done as possible to keep one day out of seven entirely restful.

In a Jewish community, or in any district where a majority of citizens wish to observe the seventh day rather than the first, provision should be made for their convenience; but in neighborhoods where a large majority wish to observe the first day, those who keep the seventh should refrain from so transacting their business on the first day as to interfere with the repose of those around them.

It probably makes no difference whatever, to health or morals, whether Saturday, Sunday or any other one day out of seven is observed as the Sabbath day, but a rest and recreation day every week is a psycho-physiological desideratum. Sabbath-keeping need not include definite religious observances; quiet picnics and excursions of various healthful and recreative kinds are not properly classifiable as Sabbath-breaking.

Rest is what toilers need, and as rest is not idleness, it is not easy to answer off-hand any question pertaining to the special feature which Sabbath observance should assume on behalf of peculiar temperaments. Church-going people number among them resters and non-resters, for what is rest to one person is by no means rest to another of different temperament and opposite requirements.

To some people two sessions of Sunday-school and two church services will constitute means of rest as well as of grace; while to other members of the same family the chief Sabbath blessing is the opportunity afforded by the rest-day for remaining in bed all the morning and taking the remainder of the day very quietly in privacy or in the open air.

A lady of our acquaintance actively employed in business as stenographer and typewriter in a public office every working-day, declared that she enjoyed absolute rest on Sundays, though she was a church singer and a Sunday school teacher. This lady went to her Sunday school at 9:30 a. m., and immediately after its session entered the church edifice and took her place in the choir for the 11 o'clock service. At 2:30 she conducted a Bible class in the school room, and at 7 o'clock she was again in the church choir for evening service. Here was active (not passive) participation in four public services on one day, yet to her that day was one of perfect rest and most refreshing tranquility.

It seems difficult, at a glance, to see how such occupation is consistent with obedience to the letter of a command which contains the injunction, "Thou shalt do no manner of work," and if it be argued that work in that sense means only labor for which people receive wordly compensation, then all Jewish and Christian ministers and professional singers, who receive salaries for services rendered on Sabbaths, are under condemnation.

To the conservative Jew, who has no loophole of escape like that of the Christian who says that Christ did away with the letter of the law of Moses, the synagogue services on Sabbaths and Festivals which give employment to professional cantors and preachers must present an enigma, unless the "sea of the Talmud" contains minute explanations of how such work is compatible with doing no manner of labor. We can see an inkling of an explanation if the technical line is drawn sharply between work and labor, and again if a distinction is made by casuists between necessary and unnecessary occupation; but until we have left all bondage to the letter, and breathed the free spirit of the Commandments, we must have recourse to bewildering casuistries and be often caught in a net of our own casuistical spinning.

It is the spirit of the Sabbath law which needs discovery, and that spirit is the spirit of most glorious liberty. The Sabbath is not a prohibition, but a privilege; not a burden, but a delight; not a debt man owes to his Creator, but a provision for his own well being. It is the monotony of toil which constitutes its greatest burden, and let the ignorant and the deluded say what they may to the contrary, periodic rest is conducive to the greatest freshness of brain and efficiency of mechanical execution.

Whenever we are kept too long and closely at any occupation we become dulled and incapable of our best exertion. Monday's work is often the best work done throughout the week, and so is the work done on the day following any public holiday, providing that holiday has been rationally celebrated.

Our protests against Sabbath desecration do not, by any means, begin and end with condemnation of such lawlessness as leads to open violation of a day's acknowledged sanctity. The day following the Sabbath is its testing day. How do you feel after your day of rest? How well equipped are you for the work to which you should go willingly, with glad alacrity, with firmer hand, with steadier nerve, with clearer eye, because of your Sabbath-keeping? To many workers in great cities a trip to the country, or to the seashore is far better than confinement in a crowded meeting house.

We are not always in the humor for hymns and sermons; we do not always need lectures upon ethics or Bible exposition. Nature in her own sweet free way spoke to Thoreau and to many other poet-artists as no church or chapel ever spoke to them. Wordsworth could never have been inspired to write his sweetest sonnets by the pews and pulpit of a conventicle. All things have their use, their place, their time, but no one thing must be so exalted as to lead to undervaluing of something else which is at least equally valuable.

The Decalogue is synthetic. It says, "Thou shalt rest." You must discover for yourself how best to rest and not enforce your rules of rest upon your neighbors. With some people church-going is a fad, a fashion; with others it is an irksome task exacted of them, not so much by God as by "Mrs. Grundy." Church attendance which is little more than fashionable Sunday dress parade is nine-tenths mummery, and it often does more to stifle than to encourage spiritual aspirations. A Sabbath to be such in reality must be a day of rest and gladness, such a day that at its close one can sing hopefully of the blessed time and state,

"Where congregations ne'er break up,
And Sabbaths have no end,"

a statement which has often conveyed to childish minds a vision of terror in place of delight, when used to define a prospect of life in the everlasting conditions of the spiritual universe.

Though the Sabbath law of the ancient Jew was a merciful provision for human welfare, and contained within it the seed of a far higher civilization than that of the nomads—to whom tradition says it was presented by Moses as one of the commandments of the Most High—it would be a low and poor interpretation of the spirit of the Fourth Commandment, which should begin and end with dissertation concerning literal Sabbath observances only.

Agricultural interests are wisely looked after by the Sabbatic year as much as personal and animal welfare is provided for by the weekly rest-day; but the "seventh day" looms large before us in its deeper meanings as the state which will be ours when we are fully regenerated. The soul works for six days or periods on its road to a perfected consciousness of what is involved within it. These six stages of evolutionary development are consummated in the seventh period, when Christ within appears as Lord of the seventh day. At that point history is entirely transcended and the mystic philosopher, rather than the historian, must take up his parable and give to the waiting multitude an exposition of the inner meaning of the Sabbath law. It is to Jacob Boehme and such divinely illumined philosophers, rather than to literalists and legalists, that we must turn for the most helpful renderings of regeneration. The third chapter of the fourth gospel records that Jesus said to Nicodemus, "Art thou a master in Israel, and knowest not these things?" during a sublime discourse upon second birth—birth from above and from within, which signifies discerning of spiritual realities.

We are not born in total depravity, but we are born into material environments which, as Wordsworth poetically tells us in his "Ode to Immortality," prevent the growing boy from continuing to enjoy glimpses of that heaven which "lies about us in our infancy."

As long as we continue exclusively devoted to things of the material world we are unaware of our interior spiritual possessions, we remain simply unconscious of our celestial inheritance. We are sons of God but we do not know it. Conversion (from the latin, *convertere,* to turn around) is to face in a new direction. It is the introductory step in the regenerating life—a new conception, to be followed in logical sequence by a new gestation, a new birth, a new infancy, a new childhood, a new adolescence, and eventually a new maturity. This is the new spiritual manhood when "Christ within, the hope of glory," will be outwardly revealed, and we shall stand face to face with eternal realities, like eagles gazing into the sun's countenance, no longer like bats and owls, blinking like the Children of Israel when Moses was urged by the people to cover his face because of its great brilliance when he had descended from the Mount.

Have we not caught while uttering these sentences some idea of the "week" of regeneration, its six working days, and its Sabbath of delight at the close? Let us see how the scale runs and how the colors of the Bow of Promise, God's rainbow sign, are typical of our own interior experiences. Here is a sevenfold scale both natural and spiritual, exoteric and esoteric, which is at least worthy of attentive consideration.

First Day—Note A. Color Red.
  Period of Conversion or new conception.
Second Day—Note B. Color Orange.
  Period of new Gestation.
Third Day—Note C. Color Yellow.
  Period of New Birth.
Fourth Day—Note D. Color Green.
  Period of New Infancy.
Fifth Day—Note E. Color Blue.
  Period of New Childhood.
Sixth Day—Note F. Color Indigo.
  Period of New Adolescence or spiritual Puberty.
Seventh Day—Note G. Color Violet.
  Period of New Maturity.

The scale of seven is so universally manifest in Nature that it is impossible for any intelligent student of natural phenomena to ignore the significance of this remarkable numeral. That most wonderful of all books of the Bible, the Apocalypse or Revelation, which lays such stress on seven is surely a Masonic document, the inner meaning of whose hieroglyphics only those initiated into the deeper mysteries of Masonry can unveil.

The seven spirits of God, the seven golden candlesticks, the seven seals of the sacred book, which only the Lamb can break, these and all other references to seven coupled with the statement that the number of the Beast is 666, (denoting physical, mental and moral incompleteness), and the many references to twelve and its multiples, clearly convince the esoteric student that the author of that amazing document was a profound spiritually inspired mathematician, one who strangely echoed the grand saying of Plato, "God geometrizes."

The Fourth Commandment grows upon us and opens up before our wondering vision endless vistas, across which no finite eye can fully peer. We begin with a rest day once a week, on which cattle as well as servants and children are to enjoy repose, and soon we are asking the meaning of God's rainbow which all souls must cross to reach Valhalla, the Scandinavian's mythologic paradise.

Doubtless when we come to keep our mystic inward Sabbath and understand experimentally the significance of our own regeneration, we shall no longer need those outward institutions which are still essential to our welfare. But let no iconoclast imagine that Nature's way is a path of destruction or demolition. We cannot liberate birds by smashing eggshells, nor can we emancipate butterflies by rending the cocoon or chrysalis out of which each must make its own way by friction; neither can we attain to a higher order of society by assailing the letter of a commandment, the inner meaning of which is certain in due course to open up its interior reality, when we are ready for higher lessons than those which our infancy permits us to appreciate.

The severe laws with which Levitical injunction surrounded the observances of the Sabbath are certainly no part of the Sinaitic precept. Multiplied traditions have tended to "make the law of none effect," as all such petty legislative enactments have been, at best, but accommodations to human weakness and "hardness of heart."

To stone a man for picking up stones on the Sabbath is no more a divine command than to stone to death an adulteress. The conduct of Jesus with Mary of Magdala should have settled the literal controversy forever in professedly Christian circles. Stones and rocks have deep interior meanings, but the superficial legalist has no eye for the beauty of a similitude, and no ear for the music of an inspired poem, so he hurls a literal flint at the head of an offender, and while engaged in merciless persecution, persuades himself that he is doing God service.

Jesus has no word of approval and scarcely a syllable of excuse for those relentless persecutors who have blasphemed the name of the Almighty, while wreaking vengeance upon the heads of all who dare to differ from them even in the matter of the pronunciation of such a word as shibboleth, or sibboleth, concerning which controversies waxed high and raged tumultuously among fanatics of antiquity.

What says the gospel concerning the Sabbath law? The disciples of Jesus do many seemingly illegal acts for which their Master refuses to rebuke them. His sweeping asservation, sublime in its magnificent inclusiveness, "The Sabbath was made for man, not man for the Sabbath," covers the whole territory of discussion. If people are hungry they have a right to eat, and even the shew-bread in the temple is none too sacred, though it is the priest's portion, for the ideal in Israel has ever been "a nation of priests," therefore both a priestly and a priestless nation it is the boast of Israel yet to be.

How singularly do fulfilments look like disappearances. There will be no educated class in a day when every citizen is educated. The high-caste Brahman will be no longer recognized when all men are acknowledged equal. The Lord's day will no longer be a seventh portion of time when all time is fully consecrated to sweet and loving service. In the New Jerusalem estate there will be no specially holy places for the whole earth will be sanctified. No more will the oasis be conspicuous when the whole region, which was once a desert, shall blossom with the lily and the rose.

The holy day, as one day contrasted with six unholy days, will be known no more when the Golden Age shall have come and the Messianic prophecies shall be completely fulfilled. The weekly rest-day is both a concession to mortal weakness and a ladder between earth and heaven, up which the toiling masses of humanity can, step by step, approach a summit of attainment where work and rest shall have grown synonymous.

A stated Sabbath suggests relief from toil, a breathing space, a vacation time, an opportunity to become better acquainted with home and garden, with choice literature, with high art and with all that lifts our thoughts above the commonplace.

What grand opportunities are often missed on Sundays! In the summer season crowds visit the parks and the seashore, and disport themselves upon the grass under kindly shade trees; but in winter when the climate in many districts peremptorily forbids much out door recreation, the hours of Sabbath—be it Saturday or Sunday, matters not—are too often wasted or worse than wasted. Religious services should be bright and inspiring and all sermons should give hope and encouragement to the toilers who need help rather than condemnation. Home life on all holidays should be especially charming, quiet, picturesque, cheery, and all else that is necessary to make "home, sweet home" something more practically real than a beautiful phrase in a sentimental ballad.

Sunday should be the brightest day in all the week for children. Toys should never be forbidden, picture books should never be under the ban, dolls should never be banished on the eve of a Sabbath. At the same time it should be the chief aim of all homemakers (God grant us many such in place of simply housekeepers) to so interweave the golden thread of ethical instruction with whatever is amusing and delightsome to the juvenile members of a household, that religious instruction shall be gently insinuated rather than abruptly segregated from the common mass of every day instruction.

On one day out of seven there should be a respite from the ordinary course of business; account books and ledgers have no place, neither have school books on a vacation day. Sunday newspapers are a doubtful benefit. Such excellent Saturday evening papers as the *Boston Transcript,* and many others which could easily be mentioned, contain much that is well adapted for Sunday reading, and even all Sunday newspapers contain much that is useful as well as entertaining.

But what is needed more than anything else by most working people (and there should be no idlers) is recreation, change of thought and employment, and this is not secured on any holiday if we drag into it the concerns and enterprises of every common day.

One day out of every ten for periodic rest was tried at the time of the French Revolution, now considerably more than a century ago, and it was found that such a division of time proved a failure. Call us conservative if you will, but we do dare in this neurotic age to lift our voice and cry out for a better observance of a Sabbath. We say nothing dictatorial about church going, bible reading, or devotional exercises of any sort, because we leave it to each one to be fully persuaded in his own mind as regards all distinctly religious or theological aspects of observance, but we do desire in clarion tones to trumpet forth the word which falls from today's hygienic Sinai, "thou shalt rest."

Rest means brain and body salvation, better qualification for rendering noble service in the community wherever and however we may be situated. Rest, not idleness, not stagnation, but recreation; moral, mental and physical liberation from the incessant grind of business and domestic servitude is today's most urgent need.

Keep your rest day as it seemeth best unto you, but whatever you do or leave undone on the one day out of seven, let rest be its keynote, and the other six days will soon witness your nobler, happier and healthier activity.

LECTURE SIX.

THE FIFTH COMMANDMENT.
"Honor thy father and thy mother."

In this commandment we have the most positive testimony to the divine idea of the perfect equality of man and woman to be found in any ancient literature. The creation story in the first chapter of Genesis tells us of Divine Fatherhood and Motherhood, and here in the midst of the Decalogue we have a plain direction to pay equal honor to our fathers and to our mothers.

Though preachers have often opposed all movements looking toward the political equality of the sexes, on the score of loyalty to the Bible, and those who never miss an opportunity to attack the venerable Book have joined in the pernicious statement that the Bible teaches the inequality of the sexes, we ask any reader who may be a novice in theology to put the obvious interpretation upon Genesis 1: 26, 27, 28, before passing to further consideration of the text of Exodus.

Get some old bibles and cut out the first chapter of Genesis, which properly ends with the first verse of the second chapter, then ask your children, one by one, to give their ideas of what this story teaches concerning the position of the sexes. People foolishly begin to study human history somewhere in the second chapter of Genesis, totally ignoring the first chapter, consequently their ethnology and theology are equally at fault.

What, think you, mean these words in the first chapter of the first book of the Pentateuch? "So God created man (humankind) in His image, in the image of God created He them; male and female created He them. And God blessed them, and God said unto them, Be fruitful, and multiply, and replenish the earth, and subdue it; and have dominion over the fish of the sea, and over the fowl of the air, and over every living thing that moveth upon the earth." Such is the text of the well-known King James version of the Bible, from which most of the passages have been taken which have been used to enforce the ridiculous and hateful dogma that woman is only God's afterthought, and was created as a mere appendage to the masculine half of humanity.

The Bible is not responsible for the brutality that unduly venerates man and heaps contempt on woman, and it ill becomes those who pose as scholars to repeat the silly blunders and obvious misquotations and misconstructions of those blind obstructionists who read their own stupidity into the biblical text by refusing to study the Pentateuch as a continuous narrative.

Say nothing about Adam and Eve, the serpent, and other characters in the Eden allegory till you have read and, as far as possible, mastered the preceding narrative which declares that humanity is in Elohim's image, and that "Ish" and "Isha" alike proceed from the Divine creative fiat.

God is our father and our mother; we are all brothers and sisters. Woe be unto us if we eclipse the divine motherhood and thus sin against the Holy Spirit, Theosophia, the Divine Feminine. The original conception of the Trinity has been completely obscured by Christian theologians who have discarded the divine motherhood. God is our Father and our Mother; the Logos is Divine Offspring.

Father, Mother and Child are the best terms in which the threefold expression of the one Deity can be revealed to human consciousness. God is our Parent. We have all one life, we are all partakers of one bounty; we live, move, and have our being in a universe governed by one law and ever giving evidence of one immutable order.

On being asked to quote a single text from the old Testament, outside the much disputed first chapter of Genesis which proclaims the equal dignity of man and woman, we unhesitatingly reply, "Honor thy father and thy mother." No greater honor is demanded for one than for the other. What shall be said of those blind leaders of the blind, who, clad in sacerdotal vestments, or robed in the black cloth of the ministerial profession, tell their benighted congregations that God is our father, but not our mother. To all such the query to propound is, Where are your proofs of man's superior sanctity! To all such misguided teachers we have only the query to propound, Where are your proofs, Oh men of darkened understanding and misleading words, wherewith you betray the divine feminine, that your fathers are purer than your mothers, your brothers more chaste than your sisters, your sons more righteous than your daughters?

This is a modern question indeed, but Sinai settled it, as it settled many another problem with which we are now wrestling, ages before the present generation of men and women came upon the stage of earth's experience—ground to solve for themselves, what no others can solve for them, the mighty problem of human life, its object and its destiny.

When the children of Israel are leaving Egypt, they must have the aid of Miriam, the sister of Moses, or they cannot be delivered, and it is her song that urges them on in the time of their greatest difficulty, and inspires them with new hope and indomitable courage when their spirit has well nigh fainted within them. The name of Miriam means resistance, and the record tells us that Miriam resisted Moses for a while, and she was stricken with leprosy, but though she was in the wrong to contend against her brother, the people could not go forward until she had been restored to health and united her force with that of the brother whom she truly respected, though for a brief season she had resented his wise counselings.

God is no respecter of persons. If a man sin, or if a woman sin, the fruit of sin is in every case redemptive penalty. Miriam is afflicted and set without the camp until she has come to reason wisely, then she is re-admitted to the convocation and becomes a bright and worthy factor in working out the deliverance of a people. When Gehazi, the servant of Elisha, sins, leprosy overtakes him, and Naaman, the Syrian captain who has been long afflicted with that terrible disorder, must wash seven times in the mystic Jordan, *i e.*, he must entirely cleanse himself from all defilements in order to be healed. A prophet can point the way, but like all modern teachers he cannot heal another man; Elisha can but show a sufferer who applies to him the way of release from error and its consequences.

In these incidents we see that man and woman are alike worthy and responsible in the sight of Heaven. There are no two laws, no double standard of morality; for as man and woman must be esteemed and honored together, so if they transgress must they be punished that they may be reformed together. There is no sickly sentimentalism in the Decalogue; no cheap gallantry or specious chivalry or aught else that demeans while it pretends to honor, and degrades while it makes believe to elevate. It is not reverence for God but dependence on brute force, and that alone, which points the envenomed arrow, which worshippers of muscle rather than of spirit ever seek to thrust into an assemblage of honest self-respecting women.

Professor Harry Thurston Peck in the Cosmopolitan magazine (June 1899) betrayed the entire animus of the social and political inequality movement. "The last appeal is always to force," says he, and in the following words says all that can be said for man's superiority. "He has the physical power to work his will, and this alone is a lasting badge of superiority." Are these the sentiments which rule the pulpit, as well as the exclusively masculine university? If so, let us cry, "Down with the pulpit," for if such be its voice, God is excluded and cruel, relentless, pitiless energy is substituted for Divine love and wisdom.

The world has known both patriarchal and matriarchal governments, but neither has proved worthy to survive. Some modern agitators have extolled woman and condemned man, but they have come no nearer to truth than those force-worshipers who adore masculine bravery and appeal to brute strength as the supreme energy. The Decalogue is balanced in its wisdom; it goes into homelife; it addresses the children individually, and says to every boy and to every girl in the household, *Thou* shalt honor *thy* father and *thy* mother.

The Fifth Commandment has quite as much message for adults as for infants. It says to husband and wife, there must be equal respect, honor, rights, and privileges. You, sir, are no nearer to God than your wife, and you, madam, are no diviner than your husband. If one is in God's image, so is the other; your interests are one, you must honor, respect, love and cherish one another. God's sanction rests on no marriage service which contains the word "obey" in one place, while it would not tolerate it in the other. Framers of some marriage services have known Paul only at his worst and his feeblest; they have not known Moses, and surely they have not known Jesus.

Women preachers are an offense to presumptuous sacerdotalism, but Jesus commissioned a woman to inform Peter as well as the other disciples that he had risen and had appeared in the early morning to the faithful watchers by the sepulchre. Take the four gospels to pieces as you will, and we challenge you to find a single word or act attributed to Jesus which exalts man over woman. To women he spake of the mysteries of the heavenly kingdom, he pleaded their cause when men unfairly accused them of participation in crimes which men had instigated, and never did he show the slightest respect for that vitiated ceremonialism which led at length to the incorporation into Jewish liturgies of the now almost totally discarded ejaculation, "I thank thee, Oh God, who hast not made me a woman."

Superficialism had so usurped the place of genuine religion before that clause entered a prayer book, that those who apologize for it today are eager to explain that men only publicly give thanks that they belong to the sex capable of performing certain high acts of ritual, but they do not boast of their moral superiority over their sisters.

Ritualism would be truly beautiful if it did not so readily degenerate into idolatry. We are such babes even today that we often need the thunder of the commandment, which for our safe-guarding is still compelled to read, "Thou shalt not make unto thyself any graven image." Aaron and the calf are preferred above Moses with the two tables of stone in his hand, but Oh, ye priest-ridden multitude, remember that Aaron makes the calf at your request out of your ear-rings, and then you worship it. Moses is coming down from the Mount today, and he will break your idols, and you will have to drink a nauseous beverage containing your trinkets pulverized. High, pure, noble metaphysical propositions are too high for many of us, but we can well appreciate ecclesiastical millinery.

We can see candles, smell incense, hear music, touch relics, and taste consecrated bread, but we do not aspire high enough to commune with a spiritual divinity. The craze of today's Spiritualism is materialization, and that one phase of modern spiritual phenomena has been more than all others the hornet in the Spiritualistic camp. Your sorrows are multiplied, oh Spiritualist, in these transitional days because you have too eagerly sought to materialize spirit rather than to spiritualize yourselves that you might hold living communion with the realm of spirit. Today's locusts are devouring your pasture lands, you are pestered with mountebanks and fleeced by impostors, and you bring it all upon yourselves in your inordinate desire to bring down the spiritual to the level of the carnal, instead of elevating the carnal till it becomes united with the spiritual.

God sends the plagues of Egypt, but all plagues are educational; not one is vindictive, not one is purposeless. The music of Sinai is a mighty anthem, a matchless symphony, a superb oratorio, a cycle of marvelous operas. Who will be the successor of Richard Wagner in the field of musical composition and take Sinai for a theme, and the Decalogue for a libretto? It is a bold proposition, but as the Passion Play at Ober-Ammergau in Germany has never been irreverent, so at Beyreuth we may yet witness a music drama with God's representative in the title role. All depends upon the treatment of the theme, whether it be awe-inspiring and uplifting or whether it be an offensive blasphemy. An inspired musician may arise to give such sublimity to the scene that the theatre shall become a veritable temple. It is very easy to travesty the Commandments and to make of a benign precept a stumbling-block in the way of youth, but let us seek to wisely elucidate them. Again and again have ignorant, selfish and domineering parents turned to the Fifth Commandment to justify their unreasonable exactions; consequently there have arisen assailants of the Decalogue who have based their assaults upon the misconduct of their own harsh and sometimes besotted parents. We need not wonder at Ingersoll's lecture on "Liberty for Man, Woman and Child," in the light of many recent experiences of parental cruelty and injustice, and as the Decalogue is a unit—one commandment fitting into the other so that no one of the ten can be logically separated from its companions— it is quite as much in accord with the spirit of this august revelation to thunder in the ears of parents "make yourselves honorable," as to cry unto the children, "honor your parents."

That is a great saying in Proverbs, "Train up a child in the way he should go." All the utterances of wise men of old in the same marvelous collection of impressive sayings concerning the "rod" of correction and chastisement, and all else that sounds harsh (if you read harshness into it out of your own harsh feelings) are just, wise, loving, and merciful if you do but let the spirit of sound counsel percolate through the sometimes dubious vernacular in which ancient thought is dressed.

Parents, you love your children, and you seek their highest welfare or you are not worthy to be their guardians and trainers. Every child is an individual and as such must be respected; yea, the Decalogue calls upon him to worship God, and only to do you honor, therefore his first duty is to conscience, to conviction, and he is to be commended if when you tell him to outrage his moral sense, to tell falsehoods for you, to be mean, tricky, and dishonest in your selfish interest, he turns sorrowfully but firmly from you, saying, "I cannot and I will not obey such an unrighteous order." You take the name of God in vain, you blaspheme the Decalogue and call down upon yourselves the retributive justice of the Most High when you box the ears of a child and flog him with a rod pickled in your own fiendishness, when you incarcerate your offspring in a dark closet or in a solitary garret with rats for companions, and for a pretense make long prayers which shall tend to your extremest condemnation.

We need "agnostics" oftentmes to expose our hideous hypocrisies, and avowed "infidels" to call us to faith in God and the practice of righteousness. Pope Leo XIII told some of his cardinals that the great French sceptic, Ernest Renan, may have been a' scourge in God's hand to lash the church into piety, seeing how far it had departed from its original integrity.

To the orthodox Christian world, we say unhesitatingly, Robert Ingersoll was one of God's hornets, and it has been all in vain that the pulpit has ranted and bullied and anathematized the arch-heretic whose very buffoonery was sometimes necessary to lacerate professing Christendom and call as with a hornet's sting a recreant institution to repentance.

Between Heron and Ingersoll supercilious kid-glove churchianity has suffered greviously, and such suffering must continue till hypocrisy is destroyed. Sinai's exterior is all we can see, and its terrific thunderings are all we can hear, until we are ready to accompany Moses into the Mount, or go with Elijah into the mystic cave.

Then when the storm has ceased and all elemental agitation has subsided, there will be heard a "still small voice," and that is the whisper from Mount Zion, the abode of beloved holiness.

Zion is within Sinai as the kernel is within the nutshell. Let us pray and work that we may deserve to hold in our hands heaven's nutcrackers. Then shall the literal shell drop away, and the sweetness and nutritiveness of the inmost meat of the nut be prepared for our continual delectation.

No parents like disrespect. Certainly they feel shocked and horrified when a little fellow standing in a window doubles up his fists, and turning to a visitor in the room says menacingly, concerning his departing parents riding off without him in a carriage, "There go the biggest pair of liars in town." Ingersoll counselled no disobedience, nor did he attack the Decalogue at any point when he related that appalling anecdote of a disappointed angry child who had been promised a ride and then left behind while his forgetful, selfish father and mother went out driving without him, leaving him to entertain a guest with a record of their mendacity. What humbug it is to ask a child to obey the Fifth Commandment when you are outraging the ninth. "Thou shalt not bear false witness" means nothing if it does not teach that to tell the truth is necessary to salvation.

No liar can enter into the Kingdom of Heaven; therefore as long as you tell falsehoods you are outside the celestial gates. Discord, ill will, deception, rebellion, and a host of ugly unclean demons infest those homes where obedience to parental rule is called for, but where that rule is a rule of wrong, not of right; of partiality, not of equity.

How much afraid many people are of anarchy; in what terror do they stand of the violence of an infuriated mob. But there would be no anarchists if the law had at all times been equitably and amicably administered.

Nihilism in Russia has been the bitter fruit on the corrupt tree of gross injustice. The present Czar, Nicholas II, is no doubt doing all he can to induce a better state of things in his wide dominions. Though we rejoice in the new prospects opening up for the Slavic race, and can see a glorious future for Siberia, we cannot expect that in a few brief terrestrial days a vast empire will be entirely reconstructed, though rapid improvements are even now in progress.

We have had patriarchates and matriarchates; the world has deified man and dishonored woman, and then turned around and glorified woman while accomplishing man's humiliation; but there will be no peace, order, harmony nor equity, until man and woman reign together and the question of social and political equality is forever settled on the firm foundation of the first chapter of Genesis, and the teaching of the Ten Commandments.

England was richly blessed for considerably more than sixty years by having for its queen a woman whose married life was a heavenly poem, and whose influence upon the home life of multitudes has been that of a ministering archangel. When a married man calls himself the entire head of the house, he is a poor half-headed lunatic. Husband and wife together constitute the head of the household; man and woman are co-equivalent co-equals, one is not a whit higher in the scale of life than the other.

Ignorant priests can quote Paul's weakest, darkest utterances, and not even interpret those in the light of the times and circumstances in and for which they were written; but great prophets with bald heads and mighty mantles, like Elijah and Elisha, without a vestige of sacerdotal assumptiveness, pronounce man and woman divinely constituted equivalents.

There is a strange beauty, a deathless fascination, in all fine portraits of the Madonna and the Holy Infant. Art today is far more to the front than fifty years ago; every home almost has now its copy of the Sistine Madonna, the Madonna of the Chair, or some other masterpiece of Raphael or one of the other immortal painters who have made womanhood appear divine on canvas. It is not idolatry to revere the beautiful and bow respectfully before the effigy of what is essentially divine.

Children must be reached through Kindergarten methods of instruction, and childlike adults must have pictorial suggestions furnished them according to their needs. That extreme reactionary Puritanism which delighted in iconoclasm, and broke in pieces all fine carved work with axes and hammers, was not penetrated with the spirit of the gospel of beauty, righteousness and love.

There is genuine gospel in Hawthorne's "Scarlet Letter," but not in the action of the relentless persecutors of an unhappy woman and her guiltless child. We approach a delicate subject when we mention illegitimate children, and we must not think lightly of any attempts to safeguard home-life against the wily, treacherous intrusions of the execrable adulterer, but we cannot purify society by undue severity, we cannot prevent the re-commission of heinous crimes by lynching Negro offenders, nor has capital punishment in any of its barbaric (or seemingly refined) shapes lifted humanity above murder or murder would not be rife today.

Suggestions to evil are made by portraits of evil; where all harsh measures fail, the law of loving-kindness proves a great success. You are parents, or you may stand in the relation of guardians to orphaned or abandoned children. You teach those children the Ten Commandments, and call their especial attention to the Fifth. Your duty is by no means finished; it has scarcely begun. Every command from Heaven is a two-edged sword, cutting both ways. If this Commandment castigates the child who disobeys, it yet more terribly afflicts the parent who is the author of the disobedience.

Filial devotion there cannot be, where parental responsibility and respectability are unacknowledged. People have travestied this Fifth Commandment shamefully, for they have read it as though it were a chord of vengeance; they have hissed it forth as though it were a fierce anathema hurled against all disobedient children when it is in truth a gracious benedictory assurance to the obedient.

No wonder the Decalogue is picked to pieces by shallow, would-be-*higher* criticizers in back-alley journalism. This Commandment is one of promise; it seems to have been formed out of the tenderness, insight and compassion of the Most High. Parents, you are summoned to the foot of Sinai, and you are often among the quakiest of all the tremblers at the base of the burning mount. You have goaded your children to disobedience and God is holding out to them a reward if they will honor you.

God is a parent. The fatherly and motherly instincts of the Eternal are breathing through the stone tables which transfigured Moses holds in his steady grasp while you are shaking like aspen leaves; you bow your faces in your hands, and hide your eyes for very shame lest your children should see your tears when the Fifth Word is addressed to them, and the voice of the law-proclaimer rises in tones of inexpressible sweetness, "Honor thy father and thy mother, that thy days may be long in the land which the Lord thy God giveth thee." If your children honor you, God will bless them, and crown them with long life and prosperity in a goodly land flowing with milk and honey. It is hard to obey you, you are so inconsistent. Papa allows what mamma forbids, and both parents are petulant and contradictory and unreasonable oftentimes. Children suffer many things at the hands of parents, and alas! there are unwelcome children in the world and our hearts must bleed for them. You have no right to tell a child not to ask questions, to do your bidding in all things, to be tamely submissive to your every just or unjust command. Sinai whispers to your children, and implores them to do you honor, and promises them a prize if they are respectful, but Sinai's thunder is for the unjust, untruthful, unloving parent, and for the unrighteous children also, for there is no distinction of age, sex, race, or color in the presence of divine legislation.

Science is God's handmaiden. Every discovery of immutable law, of inexorable order, is but a new proof of the inflexibility of the divine decrees; pitiable, indeed, is the plight of those who see only the natural Sinai, and know nothing of the spiritual Zion which is within it.

There is no respect of persons with God, there is none with Nature. There is no variableness or shadow cast by turning with the Almighty; there is none with that Natural Law which marks the incessant operation of Herbert Spencer's "Eternal Energy." Quibble about terms and dispute over authenticities if you are pedantic enough, but sceptics all believe at last when they are confronted with inexorable Sinai revealed in Nature.

All philosophers believe in Power, Force, Energy; how many believe that power is Love, that force is Goodness, that energy is Beneficence? There is a reward for righteousness as well as a penalty for iniquity. We have heard many thunders, now we must listen to whispers; the "still small voice"—is the only direct voice of the Almighty. Noise is not music, but it is an introduction to music. The sounding of the trumpet, the blast of the ram's horn, and the voice growing louder and louder has more than one significance.

Have you marked, as we have proceeded along a winding path in the vicinity of Sinai, that the echoes of the divine tones from the speaking mountain have become clearer and clearer, up till now, when we are told of prosperity and longevity as consequences of keeping inviolate a holy precept? All parents are not harsh; all commands are not grievous; many there are who have learned the wisdom in the old song,

"Speak gently, it is better far
To rule by love than fear."

There is great encouragement for all who are afflicted with rebellious children. You are good-meaning people, but you have mistaken the wrong for the right tone in addressing your offspring. You have threatened where God promises, you have been too solicitous for the letter of your law, for literal conformity with your outward wishes, when God says, "Son, give Me thy heart." All the mistakes attributable solely to misunderstanding of the right method to adopt in reaching the young, would, if piled skyward, make a mountain tall enough to obscure the heavens from the sight of the whole earth.

The story of the prodigal is suggested in the Fifth Commandment. A certain man has two sons, one remains at home and gives him no trouble, the other plunges into every abyss of abomination. Do not falter, though your son has turned out the vilest wretch in the community. Never relax your loving efforts, though his crimes are as black as the lowest hell, and have degraded him not only below swineherds, but below the hogs in the pig-pen. The Father is on the road expecting the child to return; the light is burning in the home window, the son's room is always in readiness for his return, for, says the Father, "he will assuredly come back." The whole book of Jonah is in the story of the prodigal's elder brother; the entire life of Jesus is in the father who meets his son upon the road.

Cold-hearted legal calculators object to pardons; mumblers of the letter cry shame upon the salvation of a man who was once a thief, and is now a sincere penitent. Down with it, down with it, even to the ground; may its name be blotted out and its offspring exterminated with the birth of the newborn cycle, say we of a hideous, heartless cry for vengeance upon a prodigal when God has already overwhelmed him with the destitution which works contrition. If we sin, we suffer; suffering is sin's inevitable sequence, but why do we suffer? Not for our damnation, but for our salvation. There is no anger in the heavens, no resentment in celestial societies, against the victims of self-made hells.

Be like unto the father in the story of the prodigal; let the elder brother be a type you do not intend to imitate. That elder brother, sleek, smug, self-complacent, intensely levitical, and in the worst sense Pharasaic, is today's "adder in the path." Rather be a sweet sinner than a sour saint; we can find no just fault with any novelist or dramatist who satirizes the unsaintly *"sanctified* ones."

No child is led to righteousness by a birch rod, a leather strap or a cat-o-nine-tails. Let God send "hornets" when they are necessary, but do not let us attempt to sting. We have no right to sing, "Where is my wandering boy tonight?" with the words unaltered. Why should you take it for granted, that because your son is away from home, he is drinking, gambling or carousing? Do not confess other people's sins in public, even if you believe in auricular confession to a priest in private. You have a right to confess your own misdoings to a fellow-creature, be he priest or layman, if you think you can get help from one of larger exper-

ience than your own; but let there be no more gossip-
ing and tale-bearing and suggesting evil. Love will
save when slander will plunge a weak brother into
destruction. Give your children reputations to live up
to, and when they are in doubt and difficulty, and ply
you with searching questions, be patient and remember
the text, "Come, let us reason together, saith the Lord."
Your children are human and so are you, and parents
are also children; you have parents of your own. And
here breaks in another thought—are you honoring your
parents, while you are demanding of your children that
they honor you? Have you shelved and neglected your
venerable grandparents, have you forgotten to be grate-
ful to your foster parents or to those who adopted you?

We cannot wriggle out of the Commandments. Each
one is Eden's angel with the flaming sword which turns
in every direction to guard the way to the Tree of Life.
How multitudinous are the agencies through which truth
is pouring forth its radiance upon the world today! We
commence a discourse at Sinai in Arabia, and we may
end it in a School of Suggestive Therapeutics in Chicago. Many physicians and metaphysicians at the present moment are echoing the Decalogue in their class-
rooms, at their clinics, in their private treatments.
Child culture is today the most burning of all the fiery
questions of the age. How shall I touch the depths of
goodness in a seemingly naughty girl or wayward boy?
this is the profoundest ethical query which can address
itself to any age or community. You who are teachers
must hold out great prospects of attainment in the path
of virtue; you must make virtue so attractive and declare it to be so natural (though withal so spiritual)
that as Socrates told the youth of ancient Greece, virtue
needs only to be displayed to be loved, worshipped and
glorified.

The Fifth Commandment has been called "the first
commandment with promise." We need not listen to
any more thundering, we are half way through the
Decalogue, and we ought now be prepared to hearken to
the notes of sweet assurance which breathe through all
those mighty utterances. "Thou shalt not" is more than
imperative, it is consoling, it is full of unspeakable promise. You will not kill, nor steal, nor be impure, nor
untruthful, nor covetous, for thou shalt henceforth hear
the voice within thee which says, "My yoke is easy and my
burden is light." Dwell much, oh teachers, upon the
beneficial results of a life of virtue. Threaten less and
promise more. There has been a great deluge, a mighty
earthquake, a fierce tempest, but it has subsided and
there is a rainbow in the heavens. Zion is coming into

view, and we are beginning to catch glimpses of its innumerable company of angels.

LECTURE SEVEN.

THE SIXTH COMMANDMENT.

"Thou shalt do no murder."

We have passed the bridge; we have crossed the Rubicon. The mathematician's *pons asinorum*, should now be behind us, for we have heard the promise that if we reverently give heed to divine teachings we shall soon be out of 'the wilderness and in a goodly land, which the Lord our God giveth us. Did these discourses permit of greater amplification, we should feel disposed to supplement the preceding one with thoughts on the Land Question. Single Tax or Land Naturalization could easily be discussed without the least departure from the text, "The land which the Lord thy God giveth thee," but the Cooperative Commonwealth, Utopia and Altruria, are all in the land toward which we are journeying, and we shall be fully out of the desert and over Jordan socially and industrially when we have kept all the Ten Commandments, but not earlier in our progressive history.

Many interpretations of Law in the Gospels strike us with wonderful solemnity. The Sermon on the Mount is, much of it, in the Sixth Commandment. Hear the words of Jesus on spiritual interpretation: "I am not come to destroy, but to fulfill." "Ye have heard that it hath been said, An eye for an eye and a tooth for a tooth; but I say unto you, resist not evil;" and listen to John, the most loving and therefore the most beloved of all the disciples: "Whosoever hateth his brother is a murderer, and ye know that no murderer hath eternal life abiding in him." Oh, blustering soldiers and impatient policemen, how will ye grapple with the sin of murder? Where is the gallows? Where is the electric chair which can put to death whoever commits murder in the sight of Heaven?

All human endeavors to blot out crime have proved futile. The book of Esther contains no gospel unless we peer so far below its letter that Haman, Mordecai and all the Jews mentioned therein become figurative, and the entire story is regarded as poetry, not history. Elijah, who slays the prophets of Baal must cease out of the letter and appear only in spirit transfigured with

Jesus on the mountain, in company with Moses also transfigured, before we are ready to take one real step toward genuine civilization.

The Sixth Commandment takes us back to Cain and up to heaven. Who is Cain and where is he today who asks "Am I my brother's keeper?" Abel's blood cries from the ground for vengeance, but Abel in spirit smiles from the celestial country and says, "Poor Cain, I would help you heavenward." Murder is a terrible thing; would that it were unmentionable, but the newsboys yell of it in the streets "All about the latest murder!" surely that is not biblical or archaic; it is, alas! today's Cainism. Cain and Abel are in the world at the present moment, and one is envious of the other. Joseph and his brethren are here also, and the lesser intellects are spiteful and resentful, and they dig pits and seek to destroy the "Visionary" who sees more than they see. Murder springs from jealousy; and the root cause of jealousy is a sense of one's own inferiority, coupled with malicious desire to get rid of superiority in another instead of cultivating it in oneself. Read Othello, study the disposition of Iago, and you will know ere long what Shakespeare meant when he said "Trifles light as air are to the jealous confirmation strong as proofs of holy writ."

We need tragedy still; therefore the theatre can and should be the ally of the temple. Othello is weak because he is passionate and listens to gossip; he pays heed to slander and allows envenomed tongues to prejudice him against his noble wife, the lovely Desdemona. But Emilia, Iago's consort, is a strong woman and she believes none of her husband's falsehoods, therefore, contrary to the lying slander of treacherous "society," one woman does not always believe evil of another.

The tale in Genesis of Cain and Abel is a marvelous looking glass, a perfect mirror in which we can see ourselves reflected. Give what we can or what we may we must never be jealous of others because they have made costlier offerings and more acceptable ones than we. God is never satisfied with less than blood, for blood is life, and whoever sacrifices his lamb presents his all upon the altar. Let vulgar literalists sniff the odor of burnt flesh and nauseate their hearers with disgusting histories of heathen orgies; let them declare, to their ignorant minds' content, that the God of the Pentateuch is bloodthirsty and demands a bloody oblation, but we will preach over their heads and stand on mountain eminences while they crawl in miry swamps; for to us Zion's message has been given, and blood, translated, means life, love, truth, a clean oblation, a living sacrifice.

You must give your blood to your work or your fleshly service will always prove inadequate. Perfect consecration of affection, as well as of intellect, is the offering of Abel's lamb. Cain gives only the fruit of the ground, which symbolizes merely external offerings; fruit of the hands, service of the lips, but not the love of the heart. God respects heart-service, not formal devotion. Cain is only a ritualist; Abel is a sincere lover of God and gives his all, therefore his service is acceptable. It surely should not be difficult to trace the outworking of this idea in an ancient writer's mind, though the golden thread of spiritual meaning runs through the coarse vernacular of a semi-barbaric age even as gold is found mixed with alloy whenever precious ore is taken out of the earth.

Cain is a murderer because of envy; and here he shows to the entire world of to-day the cause of modern tragedies. People often think that the cause of their failure is someone else's success. If Abel had not offered a lamb, argues Cain, the Lord would have accepted fruits of the earth because such would have been the only offering presented to Him. Get rid of Abel and then God will have to take from you the best He can get from any one, and there will be no further grumbling in heaven. So argues the modern Cain, as well as his ancient prototype. It is blasphemy, but every murderer is a blasphemer and the sin of blasphemy is to hate your brother in your heart. How can we settle our theology so as to adjust it to all present requirements? He who loves his neighbor, loves God; he who hates his neighbor, hates God. There are no mysteries in this regard except where people create them. I do not know whether the word GOD conveys or does not convey an intelligent idea to some one else's mind, but all understand the term *brother*.

We can drop theology and study sociology, and perchance with far greater advantage. There are many to-day who attribute their failures to other people's victories, and their seeming victories to someone else's defeat. Out of this false attribution grows the detestable "Every one for himself" and "Devil take the hindmost" doctrine. Selfishness is naught but perverted self-interest. It is therefore one of the supremest duties devolving upon every teacher of ethics and instructor of the young, to point out in an unmistakable manner the radical difference which forever exists between righteous self-preservativeness and unrighteous selfishness. We are all so inter-related, so intensely inter-dependent for the

commonest necessities of existence, that it must ever
prove the height of folly to seek to construct an abiding
social edifice on any other than an enlightened cooperative base. Even the excellent Ruskin Colony in Ten-
nessee has seen trouble because ·of internecine strife,
and thus one by one co-operative colonies comes to grief,
till unsympathetic spectators turn away, more fully con-
vinced than ever that, however beautiful cooperation
may be in theory, it will never prove feasible in practice. But if not, why not? High ideals and noble sentiments are surely not baseless illusions which taunt
and mock us with their beauty, while they must forever
elude our realistic grasp.

Ideals are our chief inspirers; without them we could
never mount or soar above the mediocre level of present
attainment. But to realize an ideal outwardly will
always continue impossible until it has first been realized inwardly. It is not what we think, believe, or
wish, but how we actually feel toward each other, which
is of supremest moment. Wisely indeed the book of
Leviticus commands us at first not to hate our brethren
in our hearts, and then counsels us to love them even as
we love ourselves. (Vide Lev. xix.)

The hideous crime of lynching has been defended
by many perpetrators of that grossly barbaric act,
because, say they, a warning must be given to the Negro
race through making examples of those vile men who
have committed unmentionable atrocities. There is
always something to be said in extenuation, though
nothing in favor, of a violent lawless deed when a community is aroused to what it is pleased to call righteous
indignation against iniquity; but in calmer hours, when
blood is cooler and the passion for revenge less evident,
the lynchers themselves are forced to admit that crimes
are not rendered less frequent because of such barba-
rous proceedings. Among peoples who are as yet almost
totally void of spiritual perception, barbaric retaliation
may appear like meting out simple justice without waiting for the slow process of law; but every student of
psychic phenomena and all who are giving any appre-
ciable measure of attention to the silent influential working of occult mental energies, will surely pause before
they dare to advocate the commission of a retaliatory
act which carries with it the dangerous spirit of
revenge, which will surely, somewhere, find expression
in some new act of rage or cruelty.

The worst crimes ever committed are due to
unbridled lusts or unsubdued passions, and no passion
is so dangerous as that of hate, which is love inverted
and diabolized. As love is the creative force through-

out the universe, hate, which is love's inversion, therefore its contradictory, is the arch-destroyer; consequently to let loose the fires of hate is to impose upon the very community you are seeking to protect and benefit, an efficient cause for some terrific mental cyclone. The fierce cruel cry, "Remember the Maine," which cursed American journalism during the torrid summer of 1898 was, later on, so far retracted as to its original meaning, as to be converted into some such mild and gracious utterance as "Remember the heroism of the brave lads who suffered when the Maine exploded." In that change is presented a vivid example of how greatly ashamed thinking people soon become of those rash words and deeds which, in hours of fury, seem to frenzied intellects entirely justifiable.

The chameleon-like policy of jingo journalists may fairly be looked upon as undertaken for revenue only; but the mass of the people is never moved by the mercenary feeling which may actuate the proprietor of a sensational newspaper. It is in hot blood, never in cool, that the people rise in fierce denunciation and cry out for the blood of those who have outraged them. As so many lovers of the Bible, and people who sincerely believe it to contain a divine revelation, support the practice of capital punishment by biblical texts, we respectfully request all such to weigh and ponder well the story of Cain and Abel which distinctly declares, that though Cain was an acknowledged murderer, God set a mark upon Cain so that no one who encountered him should dare to slay him. The narrative distinctly teaches that whoever slew Cain would take unto himself a portion of the murderer's curse. Here is a splendid opportunity for all who are seeking to show the consistency of Holy Writ, to rise to the occasion with such a declaration as the following: The same God, who, in Genesis revealed His will concerning the treatment of the transgressor, gave the Decalogue from Sinai, as recorded in Exodus, and among its thunders shook the world with this detonation, "Thou shalt not kill;" and again the self-same God becomes incarnate in the manifested Logos and acts out His own unalterable will in the person of Jesus who refuses to stone the adulteress, tho' adultery was a capital offence according to Mosaic legislation, but instead of murdering her, effects her conversion from adultery to sanctity.

Rev. Chas. Ames, the worthy successor of Jas. Freeman Clarke, at the Church of the Disciples in Boston, together with other good and able men in and out of the liberal Christian ministry, have lifted up their voices in no uncertain tones against the iniquity of legal murder; and it is most devoutly to be hoped that the present century may witness, among other greatly needed reforms, the total abolition of capital punishment in all civilized sections of the earth.

The pulpit, as a rule, does not lead the pew, in this respect, for it must most regretfully be admitted that a very large percentage of religious teachers still cling to the mischievous opinion that cruel retaliation will stamp out iniquity. What have barbaric punishments done up till now? *Lex talionis* has surely had a sufficient trial through all the centuries and millenniums in which people have boasted of its enforcement. An alleged remedy which has been persistently tried for so long a time and has proved entirely unsuccessful, may surely be discarded, without fear or regret, in favor of another course of action which has for one of its chief recommendations practical novelty coupled with sweet humanity. It is the fighting blow-for-blow spirit which is still the world's greatest curse.

The Dreyfus case in France which, because of the gross injustice connected with it, cast a stigma on the French Republic, which will prove very hard for the French Nation to completely obliterate, owed its entire animus to an insane idolatry of the Army. Just as king-worshippers in days of old took for their motto "The King can do no wrong!" so modern idolators of everything military, have acted as though their watchword must ever be "Our Army can do no wrong." Protect the Army at all hazards was the sentiment of the Anti-Dreyfusards throughout the trial of an innocent Jewish Captain, who would never have been convicted of any offense against his country had it not been for the resolution on the part of the idolized Army and its sycophantic worshippers, to shield the guilty by condemning the innocent rather than let it be known that the popular idol was corrupted at its core. It is a noteworthy instance in modern history, that "Down with the Jews," and "Long live the Army," have been contemporary clamors.

Jews are often soldiers and the history of the people of Israel proves them to be by no means averse to military tactics; but the undisputed history of the Jews abundantly proves that they have made grievous mistakes whenever they have sought to gain or even retain supremacy at the point of the sword. If Israel is God's especial champion, if the Jewish people must prove themselves chosen and distinguished above all other peoples upon earth, then must Israel learn that only as Prince of Peace can Messiah come to Zion. It matters not whether one's sympathies are chiefly with or-

thodox Zionists, who look forward to a literal rebuild-
ing of the city of Jerusalem and a recolonization by
Jews of Palestine in the very near future, or with those
other Jews who do not favor, geographically, Zionistic
propensities, but interpret all Messianic prophecies in
an extra-local manner; the fact remains that if the Jews
have yet a mission to fulfill on earth that mission is one
of peace, not warfare.

The typical Jew is naturally pacific; to him education
is of the utmost importance, and engagement in peaceful industries, both commercial and agricultural, is con-
genial. If the lesson of the Dreyfus case is now ade-
quately heeded, the kindred hootings of a savage mob,
"*A bas les Jnifs*," and "*Vive l'armee*," will not have been
without profound and profitable significance.

Judaism, as the mother of universal peace, may yet
be crowned by all the nations; and if such proud destiny yet awaits the scattered sons and daughters of
reviled but never conquered Israel, new and glorious
light will have been found to shine upon those glowing
prophecies of Israel's coming victories which have
cheered the hearts and kept alive the courage of millions of persecuted exiles through all the weary ages
of dispersion and affliction. Jews have sinned in common with Gentiles, and though Jew-baiters and Jew-
haters are entirely without excuse, those who are loyal
to the cause of Israel are not doing wisely if they resort to silly flattery of the Jew on every possible occasion.

To acknowledge the ideals of a people and to pay
tribute also to that people's glorious achievements in
the face of almost insuperable difficulties, is only right
and honest; but in the great cosmopolitan state of the
age to come, neither Jew nor Gentile can reign alone,
for none will be subservient where all must be co-operative.

It ever remains for *spiritual*, in contra-distinction
from *material*, scientists, to unfold the hidden treasures
of the Law and to dilate especially upon the inward
aspects of all important truth. "Lay down your arms,"
say advocates of arbitration in place of warfare, and so
say we from our avowedly and distinctively metaphysical platform, but it is all in vain that we ask the nations
to disarm until we ourselves have practiced private individual and family disarmament. The Conference at
the Hague in Holland, which has already borne good
fruit in many noticeable ways, cannot accomplish by
means of its deliberations anything like so much as its
most enthusiastic promoters and admirers hope it may
accomplish, because the roots of warfare lie deep

within our individual hearts, and we do not as a rule seek to eradicate them. There is always something attractive and impressive in a brilliant assemblage of dignitaries from various parts of the world, gathered to consider ways and means for the general betterment of human conditions; but there is also much of picturesqueness in military tournaments, and nothing can appear better dressed on the occasion of a patriotic celebration than a good-sized cannon. We must beware lest we permit ourselves to be over-charmed with glittering externals and while paying homage to those, forget the weightier matters of the Law. Men fight duels over trifles; nations go to war like peevish children to resent trivial insults and petty aggressions. The war spirit is after all the puerile spirit; the peace spirit is a matured spirit.

Children are fascinated with uniforms, so are all shallow adults. No games are more popular than those played with toy soldiers. Sham fights in which real soldiers amuse the multitude on public occasions are among the most popular diversions in various parts of England, and though no harm is done to any one, for the entire celebration passes off peacefully, no psychologist can fail to see that even such spectacles create in the minds of thousands of susceptible young people an admiration for warfare, which is probably also entailed upon a succeeding generation. One of the greatest difficulties in the way of abolishing or even reducing the great standing armies of Europe is the intense admiration for military display exhibited by the rank and file of taxpayers, upon whose usually slender resources a very heavy drain is constantly being made to support impressive military pageants. We all know the parrot cry of "Expansionists" and "Imperialists," that Divine Will ordains that the Caucasian race should completely dominate all inferior races; but even though this surmise be true, the greater a people and the wiser, the more pacific should be its course of action. Neither the British Empire nor the United States of America can stand free of blame in the light of the Sixth Commandment. It is utterly useless to sing constantly in church, as a response to each commandment, "Incline our hearts to keep this law," if we do not desire our hearts to be so inclined, or if we do not voluntarily co-operate with divine goodness in so inclining them.

The Sixth Commandment has always been very imperfectly observed, and were it carried out in anything like its obvious fullness, it would be the rallying cry of all civilized peoples united to abolish war. Dr. Lyman Abbott, and other able preachers of the advanced school in American Congregationalism, move very cautiously along the road which leads to eventual declaration of universal peace; but there are some intrepid souls who are even now ready to declare that the hour has already struck for firing the last cannon or participating in the last military show. Our good friends, the Vegetarians, are very apt to extend the meaning of the command, "Thou shalt not kill" until it has embraced more than the human world, and though there are decided extremists among them, who are at present open to the charge of impracticability, there can be no doubt in the minds of enlightened evolutionists as to the final solution of the diet problem. Though it is not safe to say that we should all grow spiritual and humane at once did we desist from eating meat, it is a psycho-physiological fact that flesh-eating does tend in the direction of warlikeness. As we become increasingly peaceful in our desires and thoughts we shall advance gradually but surely to a far more beautiful and a much healthier mode of eating than generally prevails at present.

Slaughter houses are not true adjuncts of civilization, and if it be discovered and demonstrated that we can all live better without animal food than with it, we may joyfully hail the day when the Sixth Commandment will be observed in all its fullness; and men and animals shall share the planet together as friends and comrades even as Isaiah and other great Prophets have foretold. First and last, however, is it the paramount duty of the teacher of ethics to put this whole vast subject on a solid metaphysical foundation.

Let us emphasize continually in homes, schools, and business houses the great need of feeling kindly one toward the other; then, as surely as the law of cause and effect works undeviatingly, out of our good interiors will spontaneously proceed kindly words and actions, and society will be fully regenerated by the loving practice of all that is inculcated in the Golden Rule. "Whatsoever ye would that men should do to you, do ye even so to them."

LECTURE EIGHT.

THE SEVENTH COMMANDMENT.

"Thou Shalt Not Commit Adultery."

Though a single word only is used in the literal text of the Seventh Commandment, it is almost universally admitted that far more than the obvious meaning of this one word is implied in the comprehensive spirit of the Decalogue. The purity of the marriage relation and strict conformity to the monogamic rule has ever been one of the leading glories of the House of Israel.

Polygamy and polyandry, as well as slavery, were in the world, even as human sacrifice was in the world when the bright light of dawning Judaism awakened the consciences of multitudes eventually,—though only of a few at first,—to discern the breaking of a new and glorious day of human liberty and purity. Chastity and freedom are inseparably connected, for there is no slavery so gross, no chain so binding, as that of ungoverned sensual appetite.

Human beings are called upon by the trumpet voice from Sinai to rise to heights of moral grandeur, unknown to them before, and as they rise they become increasingly a sacred and peculiar people, unlike those around them, because of practical superiority in thought, word, and conduct.

The Sermon on the Mount takes the Seventh Commandment in hand, just as it takes all the others, and transfers our thought from the outward letter to the animating spirit.

Such a saying as "Whosoever has desired to commit adultery has already committed the offense in his heart," may be a hard doctrine in many ears, but all metaphysical reasoning must fall instantly to the ground if such a saying he rejected. Times without number the world's greatest prophets have called upon the people to practice inward cleanliness; purity of heart, virginity of desire, freedom from the will to act impurely, these have been the hidden virtues which seers (who look below all surfaces) have unanimously counseled and extolled.

Of what avail is hypocrisy? How can the fountains of life (will and thought) be polluted and the externals of speech and action be made pure? Only as the interior of the "cup and platter" are cleansed and kept wholesome can we reasonably hope for purity in outward life.

It is now being very generally conceded by all deep thinkers, that the psychic influence exerted by and through the mother upon the unborn child has most of all to do with shaping the interior mold into which the living entity is cast prior to the completion of gestative processes. Though all souls are alike in primal essence, and every human being is divine at core, we have to confront the exteriors of existence both psychically and physically at every turn while journeying through the world, and as the Ten Commandments are surely given as a rule for human practice, and all are directly concerned with our mutual duties and obligations here and now, we are specially interested in tracing out their immediate relations to those vital metaphysical teachings, which an ever increasing multitude regard as the only certain light which points a way through the present wilderness, out of sensuous "Egypt" into spiritual "Canaan."

We are all working our continuous Exodus out of the state where we have long been living upon the contents of Egyptian flesh pots, to where we shall happily and healthily subsist upon the delicious and luscious fruits of that Land of Promise, which is still the ideal unattained, though an ideal attainable. As we press toward our goal, which means for us nothing less than complete subjection of flesh to spirit, we hear the Commandments within ourselves ringing out one by one with ever increasing distinctness, because as we evolve spiritually the voice of God in our ears grows ever louder and clearer.

At first there is no higher or deeper meaning attachable by us to the Seventh Commandment than an earnest counsel to live decently and respectably in the family relation, to observe a code of honor and obey the Golden Rule as far as we understand its import in all marital or conjugal relations. But as we grow more illumined, we begin to see the futility, almost the impossibility, of faithfully observing an outward law if our thoughts and affections are permitted to disobey it. Nine-tenths of the degrading sensuality actually existent in the world today is an almost inevitable outcome of the mere externalism in religion and morals which has satisfied itself with the semblance of outer conformity to a divine precept, the interior sense or meaning of which has remained entirely unexplored.

All spiritual education aims upward; all true educators place the highest possible standards as ideals before their disciples. Through constant meditation or concentration of thought upon these sublime spiritual pictures, the lower desires which are common to the animal plane of human consciousness are overcome because they are transcended, and by this means a physiological as well as a psychological transformation is effected within the individual. All questions pertaining to generation are carefully veiled and surrounded with an atmosphere of speechless mystery in what is termed "polite society," and it is well that this should be so until the sacred question of reproduction can be dealt with in a far loftier and sublimer way than is customary among those who either appeal to lasciviousness or else take an altogether too austere and often terrifying view of a question which only needs delicate, luminous, scientific handling to render it acceptable to all earnest philanthropists, who, if they think at all, must agree, that what most nearly concerns the perpetuation of the human family ought to be dealt with wisely and courageously.

The Jews as a people have enjoyed for many centuries a well-earned reputation for unusual fidelity in the marriage relation, and wherever strict Judaism prevails, one is pretty sure of finding a far greater than average degree of domestic peace and happiness. The usual orthodox or conservative Jew is a man who attends strictly to business in business hours, but who always finds time for the enjoyment of family life when he has left his shop or office. In London and other large cities where Judaism has its strongholds, the inner life of Jewish households compares more than favorably with the domestic peace of non-Jewish families.

We hear much today concerning "The new woman," both *pro* and *con*, but in all her beautiful and desirable aspects, we find her fully described in the thirty-first chapter of Proverbs. The charming composite picture of ideal womanhood drawn according to tradition by Solomon's son Lemuel who seeks for his son a proverbially and exceptionally excellent wife, may be fairly regarded as a typical Jewess of the fairest and noblest type, alike ancient and contemporary.

Success vs. failure in marriage must be the outcome of mutual appreciation and mutual understanding. Much that commonly passes for love is no true affection, but simply passional impulse, unenlightened by reason. Co-education, which places boys and girls on a proper equal level, has much to do with educating the average youth and maiden above that foolish and dangerous prudery which, though masquerading as the grace of modesty, is often nothing but an artful cover for the most shameless views of sex relationship entertained in secret.

The intelligent teacher and practitioner of spiritual science studiously avoids all suggestions which even remotely border on pruriency, and though every intelligent person knows that there are certain natural distinctions between men and women adapting each and all to varied works of usefulness in the economy of universal order, all such vulgarity as discourses on "sex-magnetism" or the alleged desirability of healer and patient being always of opposite sex is rigorously excluded from all genuine metaphysical curricula.

The New Testament teaches that "in Christ" there is a new creation. The old order is surpassed, and a new regenerate order takes its place. As we are none of us fully regenerated, though we may be all in process of regeneration, it behooves us to move intelligently in our instructions, along a road which surely, though it may be but gradually, leads from the old to the new in human perception, and thence into corresponding practice. For the great majority of men and women a celibate life may not be commendable, though individual celibates may be very noble.

There is a right and proper regard for the sacred offices of paternity and maternity in the hearts and minds of a very large percentage of approximately normal human beings, and were it not for false standards and corrupt social usages sanctioned by "Mrs. Grundy," there would be far more happy marriages and far healthier children than abound at present.

Far too much stress is usually laid upon the fact of sex difference, but this is happily being rapidly overcome by the certain adjustment of the relations of men and women through the spread of a wiser education than formerly prevailed. A double standard of morality is fast falling into disrepute; and, while woman cannot permit herself to indulge in that degrading license which man has too long considered legitimate for his own sex, though unlawful for the other, it is possible to so rear boys and girls together that a common goal of untarnished purity shall be the ideal of all.

If we wish to truly raise the standard of morals, we must not accentuate sex differences as they have been accentuated in days gone by. Men and women must enjoy good comradeship, and go about together on equal instead of unequal terms. In the interests of morality we must certainly put in a plea for the total discontinuance of all those practices which make young women degradingly dependent for amusements and suppers on young men. Two young people can go to a lecture, concert, opera, or any respectable entertainment together without a chaperon, even though one is a youth and the other a maiden, but they should go as equals, financially as well as otherwise. Two young men or two young women can go about together on equal terms of share-and-share-alike, the result being that mutual esteem and abiding friendship is fostered; but wherever one is financially dependent on the other, the one who pays the bills becomes "bossy," while the one who is always "treated" becomes servile.

Marriage is properly a copartnership of equals, and unless both feel this there will always be the assumed headship of one and slavishness of the other. The best thinkers of today are not in favor either of a patriarchate or a matriarchate, but as Felix Adler and other brilliant speakers on Ethical Culture platforms have declared, man and woman are co-efficients; the head of the ideal house is dual, not single.

Man and woman will naturally assume right mutual relations when false beliefs are conquered and true ideals upheld. Not only is it necessary to insist upon financial equality and other commercial as well as educational aspects of the sex question, it is still more momentous a theme when we come to suggest the antidote to all prevailing false feeling concerning virtue and its propagation; this needs vigorous as well as careful handling.

Gertrude Campbell, the author of a beautiful poem, "Non-resistance," quotes as a heading for her verses, "Resist not evil," and "He who wars with sin leaves nothing lovely in his earthly tracks." With the first text we are all so familiar that it falls unchallenged on many ears; it is accepted as a trite saying to be tacitly endorsed because of its alleged divine origin, though to put it into actual practice, is very far removed from the intention of a majority of "pious Christians" who seem to consider this counsel an impracticable portion of divine revelation. Strange inconsistency to profess to know better than the Omniscient! The second motto will certainly be severely contested wherever quoted, because it is not supposed to be fortified with any specially divine sanction. Let us consider it in relation to the Social Purity Question one in which we ought to be all deeply interested. It has been wisely said that when vice is first beheld it appears hideous and repels us by its ugliness, but when we have gazed upon it a number of times we are apt to grow so accustomed to its distorted lineaments, that we fail to feel any longer our original repugnance for its deformity.

Blind leaders of the blind, well-intentioned though they often are, instead of explaining the path of virtue and making that path attractive, fall into the baleful error of describing vice in all its details on the specious plea that familiarity with vice is security against its snares.

Temperance workers are, many of them, beginning to get their eyes open to the fact that boys have learned to run a distillery, and have often been known to manufacture whiskey through following directions received from a temperance lecturer in a church, who was warning his hearers against the sin of drunkenness. Many a "converted crook" has led young people who have attended "revival meetings," into all the secrets of crookery by telling the public all about his own career while yet an unconverted man.

We want no lectures on vice to young or old of either sex, but the world can always be benefited by dissertations on the path of virtue. The Brahmins, at all events those among them who steadfastly adhere to the beautiful spirituality which is the essence of original Brahminism, teach that if we would attain to the Nirvanic state of rest and bliss united we must contemplate only the Divine, and so concentrate our mental gaze upon the pure ineffable, that we shall be weaned away from all the allurements of those lower planes which, according to Occultism, are always ready to capture those who meditate upon them. Swedenborg's entire system of philosophy trends in the direction of "turning to the Lord," and thus "overcoming the hells." All who know Swedenborg well enough to have read his much-controverted treatise on *"Celestial Love and Its Chaste Delights, also Adulterous Love and its Sinful Pleasures,"* though they may not think the whole of that volume desirable for children's reading, cannot fail to see how a great philosopher, grappling with actual conditions prevailing in Europe in the middle of the Eighteenth Century, clearly pointed out the distinction between lesser and greater evils, and clearly taught something resembling the famous saying, "Of two evils always choose the lesser," though he aims from first to last to fix the reader's thoughts and affections upon the sublimest ideal of celestial conjugal relationship.

True marriage has been in high degree practically illustrated by England's hallowed Queen Victoria, who, after the passing to unseen realms of Prince Albert in 1860, lived so far above the thought of a possible second marriage that she went *extremely* far in manifesting disapprobation of what Church and State alike sanction—the remarriage of widowers and widows. There are many subjects which do not readily lend themselves to elaborate verbal analysis, and this is surely one of them. No one can read the Pentateuch and then the Gospel without clearly tracing the Sinaitic tone in the first, "Thou shalt not commit adultery," and the Zionistic voice in the second, "In the resurrection (or regeneration) they neither marry nor are given in marriage, but are as the angels." But how are the angels? many will inquire. We must become angelic ourselves before we can fully answer that question; but Jesus evidently alluded to the well known Kabalistic view of angels when he replied to the Saducean lawyers who questioned him as to whose wife in the spiritual state a woman would be who on earth had lived with seven lawful husbands, for six times had she become a widow. The only counsel which will surely stand the test of all experience is that which urges perfect fidelity in thought, word and deed to the highest standard of virtue already perceived.

"Man grows as higher grow his aims," is a good motto; and if for the word *aims* we substitute *ideals,* we shall meet the uttermost requirements of transcendental philosophy.

If we question Emerson, he will tell us in his wonderfully sublime essay, "The Oversoul," that the way to triumph over all lower propensities, is for the as-yet-imperfect human intellect to adore its own essential and potential perfectness. "I, the imperfect, adore my own perfect," is an unsurpassed saying, for it has in it the richest cream of all the grandest philosophies extant.

Now let us consider the richest and most assuring tone in the seventh Word from Sinai which we will read thus: Thou, Oh spiritual Israelite ("he is a Jew who is one inwardly") shalt appear in the eyes of all men as unusually pure, for though thou travelest and sojournest among adulterers, thou shalt not commit adultery thyself; and thou shalt learn how to extirpate adultery among those who yet commit it. This is thy mission, for this thou art called to be a peculiar people, Oh Israel!

As we grow to be sinless in any respect, we can reform those whom the special sin we have conquered has engulfed. "Let him that is without sin cast the first stone." The immaculate Christ alone can cast it, and in his hand it is a truth presented in love. Magdalene dies to sin and is awakened to righteousness because Jesus has stoned to death her frailty, and awakened within

her a loving, quenchless determination to be henceforward pure and strong.

Zion again is found within Sinai, and though the letter would kill, the spirit points the road to life immortal.

LECTURE NINE.

THE EIGHTH COMMANDMENT.

"Thou Shalt Not Steal."

Among the numberless Shakespearian quotations with
which modern writers continually enrich their essays,
none is more popular and none more thought-provoking
than the following magnificent lines from "Hamlet."
  "This above all, to thine own self be true;
      And it must follow, as the night the day,
    Thou can'st not then be false to any man."
The same author has also familiarized us with the
grand heroic sentiment for honor, expressed in the
equally well remembered words, "He who steals my
purse steals trash." It is not altogether complimentary
to present-day civilization, or to contemporaneous standards of morality, to cull too freely from the pages of
dramas written more than three hundred years ago, if
we are keen at contrasting the glorious contempt for
mere external wealth contained in many of them with
the slavish idolatry of gold now, alas! so terribly conspicuous. But though a first glance may serve to set us
to thinking soberly and perhaps gloomily upon the
degeneracy of this present age, we soon begin to consider wisely that the high standard of nobility set by
the greatest seers and poets of the time of Queen Eliz-
abeth, were far more truly ideal conceptions of prophetic geniuses than samples of prevailing practice
and opinion. We may with certainty decide that there
have been, as there still are, great souls who shine like
beacons in the midst of surrounding moral darkness like
stars on a winter night, but never does history inform
us that the great mass of slowly evolving humanity has
risen to a height where the sublime ideals of the prophets and sages have been actually embodied in the common lives of the multitude.

We shall never take in the true meaning and message of the Decalogue unless we remember that the Ten
Commandments were given from a mountain summit,

a spiritual eminence far above the ordinary table-land on which the great percentage of "respectable" people are living even to-day. We have not grown up to the Decalogue, but we are steadily growing toward it. An immense gulf yet yawns between the supreme altitude of the Zion-height to which the Sinaitic moral code is ever pointing us, and "conventional morality" as taught and practiced today.

Tradition says that thirty-four hundred years have elapsed since the days of the historic Moses, and modern critics of the book of Exodus inform us that all the Ten Commandments are much older than the date usually assigned for the Sinaitic revelation, for though they may have been put together into a solid body of precepts at that time, they can be found scattered here and there in ante-Jewish literature, just as all Christian maxims which are formulated into a solid body of teaching in the Sermon on the Mount, can be found scattered freely through the Jewish literature from which much of the New Testament doctrine was confessedly compiled. It is quite as useless for a devout Jew to insist upon the exclusively Jewish origin of the Decalogue as it is for a pious Christian to claim originality for all the sublimest ethical inculcations to be found in the gospel narratives.

Truth does not depend on any age or place. All great teachers have declared truth to be divine, immortal, universally accessible, and therefore in no sense private property or a proprietary article. There may be such a practice as filching or plagiarizing when it comes to reproducing sentence by sentence, the words of a predecessor or a contemporary in exact literary form, but ideas, like principles, are universal. No one can claim to have actually originated any truthful utterance; the author of Ecclesiastes may have been well within the line of reason when he wrote, "There is nothing new (absolutely) under the sun." The gross valuation placed upon money, as such, is responsible for perhaps ninety per cent. of the stealing which abounds today without any such cause as lack of material necessities to extenuate it.

We may well agree with those philanthropists who excuse theft where a poor woman steals bread to save her children, more than herself, from positive starvation, but there is no excuse for those robberies and defalcations, of which we so frequentlyy read, where persons who have stolen on a large scale have long received ample wages to supply them with the comforts as well as necessaries and decencies of existence. It is ever the province of the genuine psychologist (and every teacher should be well versed in the fundamentals of practical psychology) to point a needed moral by getting behind effects to causes, thereby discovering a radical and thoroughly effective remedy for the disease of dishonesty, and every other moral ailment which afflicts society. With the constant advance of polite terminology we are growing further and further away from the strong old custom of calling a spade simply a spade, therefore we like the fine technical terms "kleptomania" and "kleptomaniac" much better than the old-fashioned thief and theft. There is a bright and also a dark side to the employment of these Greek euphemisms. The bright side consists in the growing tendency among criminologists, penologists, jurists and all who are called upon to deal with crime directly, to abandon harsh views and practices in favor of milder doctrines and gentler usages. The dark side is the tendency to excuse criminality on the score of constitutional incapacity for virtue, a tendency which weakens moral fibre and counteracts the good effects which might reasonably be expected to follow upon a kinder mode of dealing with offenders than has been hitherto thought practicable.

Dishonesty is clearly an affliction of the will, a concomitant of perverted desire on its subjective side, while on its objective side it is merely the inevitable fruitage of illicit ambitions. It is not credible that so long as mere external wealth is idolized, and the leading question everywhere asked concerns what a man has rather than what he is, young men and women with no very strong moral principle will miss an opportunity of thievishly appropriating to themselves whatever they can lay hands upon which, in their belief, will raise them in the estimation of members of that society in which they most desire to move. Moral principle is certainly not being sufficiently evolved in the churches and religious schools which fashion patronizes. No one has yet written a reply to Edward Bellamy's two magnificent novels, "Looking Backward" and "Equality," wherein he distinctly proves that the chief motive for dishonesty could not exist in such a social state as he has depicted with a master hand in both those marvelous romances. The unanswerable argument against valuing people because of what they have, instead of on account of what they are, is based upon the undeniable fact that stolen money has just as great a purchasing power in every mart of trade as money obtained by honest industry. Aristocrats, who cling to their ancient motto, *noblesse oblige,* may yet have a part to play in social elevation; but plutocrats who can lay no other claim to distinction than the possession of so many million dollars or pounds sterling, can only offer a ludicrous spectacle in the eyes of all merit-respecting persons.

We are no champions of poverty, though we do not overlook the intelligible theological distinction between voluntary poverty and involuntary destitution. "Sell all thou hast (or as Marie Corelli translated it in 'The Sorrows of Satan,' sell half thou hast) and give to the poor," can easily be made to signify that we should overcome poverty in others as a result of our own opulence without doing the slightest violence to the spirit of the text. But reason clearly proves that there can be no giving or distributing where there is nothing to bestow, and common honor insists that no one can have a right to give away other people's property.

A recommendation to honesty is a counsel to industry, for idleness and destitution must ever go hand in hand and destitution will surely lead to theft or suicide. Nature provides superabundantly for the maintenance of a very much larger population than this planet is now called upon to support. Eighty million is now regarded as a fair estimate of the population of the United States of America, and a very small population it is, considering the immense territory included in the national area. It has been computed that ten times and even more than twelve times the present population need not result in over-crowding, but extremely good management would have to prevail in order to comfortably sustain so great a multitude.

Fear of want leads to dishonesty, no matter on what plane the fear or the want may be expressed. Poor starving creatures who pilfer in order barely to exist are at the foot of a long ladder, whose bottom rungs only appear disreputable. A little further up the same stairway we encounter the timid truckling millions who dare not avow their honest faith religiously, politically, or any other way because their "bread and butter" is at stake. A little higher than the vulgar average, we find on the same ladder, preachers, college professors and a whole host of literary and artistic people who dare not say their honest say, because salary, promotion or some other material claim is so far fettering their spirits that they are practically living a lie, and they know it; indeed, they frequently admit it. On the same ladder, also, are all who cheat tailors, dressmakers, milliners, upholsterers, caterers, and tradespeople of all descriptions more or less extensively, because they must keep up style and live fashionably, though it takes downright cruel dishonesty to keep up such deceitful appearances. The church as an institution, regardless of denomination, could do an immense amount of good if it would only publicly and unitedly veto the senseless and immoral love of display which turns today's alleged sanctuaries into something little better than "dens of robbers." The New Testament deals mercilessly with hypocrites, and even makes hypocrisy a worse offense than any other iniquity.

Hypocrisy is the basest and most nearly incorrigible form of dishonesty, because it "steals the livery of heaven to serve the devil in." Silk dresses and frizzed hair are of no avail in education or religion, but in too many a Sunday School those children who wear velvet coats, lace collars, and other fripperies of stupid fashion, are looked up to by teachers as well as classmates, while honest moderation in attire is met with a sneer of contempt aimed at something ignorantly styled poverty. A great many mistakes have been made by avowed metaphysicians during the past twenty years, in their endeavors to conquer poverty, and we are very happy to find that many extreme Mental Scientists are now walking along a truly moral track by counseling all their readers and students to set to work to build up their characters, to evolve their true individuality before seeking to draw to themselves external things to which they may not yet be fairly entitled. Instead of seeking to get something from without, we must first seek to evolve or develop some force from within, which, when sufficiently aroused and liberated, will assuredly constitute us magnets to draw to ourselves all necessary and even beautiful externals. "Seek ye first the kingdom of heaven and its righteousness, and all these (external) things will be added unto you," is a truly scientific counsel, because no sooner do we actually become great within ourselves than we begin to attract external correspondences agreeing with our interior state. It is clearly dishonest to expect something for nothing; the very desire to accrete to ourselves what we have not earned is a demoralizing mental enterprise.

Dishonesty can never be confined to mere taking of money, trinkets, or aught else that may be classed as portable belongings. Every wish to subsist on what Henry George has called "unearned increment" is thoroughly dishonest, and those who avail themselves of every possible opportunity to get something for nothing,

—even though that something be instruction or mental treatment,—are sinning grievously against their own moral, mental, physical, and circumstantial development. It may not sound highly ethical to quote the trite proverb, "Honesty is the best policy," but it is sound at the core, for though a truly honest individual is not actuated by sordid motives of worldly policy, it is perfectly fair to tell the truth concerning all roads to success, adapting our teachings to the present planes of comprehension manifested by those to whom we seek to convey instruction. Though we abhor a grasping greedy policy, and can conceive of little that is much more despicable than taking all advantage possible of a neighbor's dire necessity, there are two more points from which the vast question of honesty must be regarded. Every one condemns usury, and because Shylock is represented as a usurer in *The Merchant of Venice*, very little sympathy usualy goes out to this, by no means truly typical, Jew of the European Ghetto.

Shakespeare ended that particular play very unsatisfactorily, if he wrote it for the purpose of teaching a great moral lesson, which we are inclined to doubt after witnessing such supremely moral tragedies as *Macbeth*, *Othello*, and *Hamlet*. If, however, the playwright's intention was to hold the mirror faithfully up to European manners and customs in his day, he certainly produced a masterpiece intensely valuable to this day as a historic picture of how the average Christian felt and acted to the Jew before the advent of what we may truly call a new and higher humanitarian sentiment. Ostensible religion does not always counsel honesty; on the contrary it is often pleaded as an excuse for the commission of the grossest injustices. We do not blame religion as it is blamed by some, for we are not gullible enough to believe that any higher motive than sordid self-interest leads to Anti-Semitism. The conviction of an innocent man, like Captain Alfred Dreyfus, to five years' solitary confinement on Devil's Island (well named) and a host of other infernal acts of shameless turpitude,—all of which can be glossed over by sleek hypocrites if they can only make their dupes believe that in persecuting unoffending Jews they are protecting the church of Christ, are examples of undisguised immorality masquerading as religious impulse. What an utterly corrupt institution—corrupt as the French army has been—a church would be if it really needed such detestable dishonor and such pestilent mendacity to save it from inevitable downfall.

To steal man's honor is always worse than to filch his worldly possessions. Such was the teaching of the incomparable Bard of Avon, more than three centuries ago; but how many people really act as though they believed this to-day? Slander, malicious gossip, and every form of evil-speaking is freely indulged by canting church-members and non-church members alike, who would not hesitate to fully endorse the letter of the old rhyme,

> "To steal a pin it is a sin.
> Much more to steal a larger thing."

Seeing, then, that "he who filches my good name" is supposed to commit no sin at all, a good name instead of being, as the author of Proverbs considered it, of more value than the finest gold and the most precious gems, is regarded as of less importance than a common hairpin or some other paltry utensil, the market value of which is entirely insignificant. Though it is indeed vulgar, ill-mannered and to an extent immoral, to take even the smallest article of another's property, venial indeed in the sight of Heaven must be the offense of taking a few coppers out of a money box, when weighed in God's balances with the dastardly offense of robbing a fellow-being of honest reputation. People who take notice of anonymous letters and believe their contents to others' detriment, and all who give ear to slanderous reports of their neighbors—miserable slavish worshippers of the false God, "they say"—are guilty of sin against the Eighth Commandment; and if they presume to call themselves admirers of Shakespeare, some day he or another sincere moralist may rise up in terrible judgment to testify against them.

Jesus never turned men out of the temple precincts because they bought and sold within the sacred enclosure, but solely on account of their dishonest traffic, else how could the words apply, "Ye have made it a den of thieves." Many and blind and ingenious have been the attempted explanations of that heroic scene in the life of the great Master which immediately preceded the closing tragedy of his earthly ministry. Dr. Franz Hartmann in his "Jehoshua, the prophet of Nazareth," has so utterly misconstrued the scene as to greatly impair his authority as a judicious critic, for he has gone so far as to say that Jesus lost His temper, and with loss of temper lost His previous magical power, which loss culminated in his ignominious crucifixion. Far otherwise do wise commentators interpret the thrilling narrative. One young man unarmed, therefore seemingly defenseless, enters into the midst of a gang of hypocritical, dishonest traders, and by force of spiritual authority alone ejects them from the desecrated place. Why do they allow themselves to be expelled when they are many and He is only one? Why do they not snatch the knotted cord out of His impetuous hand and force Him out, while they remain in undisturbed occupancy? The sole answer which can be reasonably given to this most pertinent enquiry is the all convincing and ever present one, that physical strength or numbers can never prove a match for indomitable spiritual energy.

The successors or lineal descendants of those perfidious money-changers are to be met with at the present day anywhere and everywhere among Jews and Christians equally. If the scene is laid in ancient times, when every devout Jew was called upon to visit the literal Jerusalem three times a year, to offer sacrifices at Passover, Pentecost and Tabernacles, animals and birds must figure in the narrative; but today and in other lands than Asia Minor, prayer books, hymnals and indeed sittings in a church or synagogue would answer just as well for illustrations.

A large orthodox Jewish congregation in Manchester (England) some time ago passed a resolution not to admit usurers to membership; just as many Christian congregations are not willing to admit liquor sellers to the communion. Usury is not Jewish, drunkenness is not Christian, though many professors of either religion may be found guilty of one or both of these offenses. Suggestive therapeutists, who are now very much in evidence, declare that mental treatment should be first of all moral treatment; therefore, cases of thievish proclivity can be undertaken just as readily and treated quite as successfully as cases of more ostensibly physical disorder. Though present false social standards, and generally loose business ethics, have much to do with sanctioning and fostering dishonesty, it is always a vain attempt to seek to move the large social or mercantile world, *en masse* seeing that all worlds are composed of units, but individual regeneration is a work in which we can all intelligently engage. Utterly useless must it ever prove to treat people against the act of stealing so long as they desire to cheat their fellows. We must strike in this, as in all other instances, at the root of the noxious tree. We are entirely out of conceit with those reformatory barbers who use scissors, clippers and razors upon the hair of iniquity. Nothing short of a scientific depilatory which kills the root of a spurious growth can be of any solid benefit to humanity.

Spiritual methods of treatment are in every case essentially radical, dealing with causes, not with effects, except resultantly. Precisely as it is with impure thoughts, which surely manifest sooner or later in external offenses against chastity, so it is with dishonest ambitions. The Ninth and Tenth Commandments follow close upon the Eighth, and it must ever prove extremely difficult, if not impossible, to strictly observe one, if we sin against any of the others.

Again, let Sinai's trumpet cease to sound, and bid Zion's music greet our listening ears, for when we hear the new song or the old song with the new tone, "Thou shalt not steal" will convey to us the blissful confident assurance that we have reached a height where love of honesty entirely pervades our nature, and henceforth 'all thoughts, words, and acts of dishonor will have lost all fascination for us.

Let us examine ourselves searchingly, and cast out every lingering remnant of dishonest desire to profit by our neighbor's loss; then will reciprocity, not competition, be proved the law of true prosperity and the life of industry and honest love will manifest itself throughout the world in honest speech and trading.

LECTURE TEN.

THE NINTH COMMANDMENT.

"Thou Shalt Not Bear False Witness Against Thy Neighbor."

Were we called upon to choose but one chapter from the entire Bible, from which to select the most abundant moral counsels, we might feel inclined to choose Leviticus xix. This marvelous repository of the sublimest Jewish ethics says, "Speak unto the Children of Israel, saying, ye shall be holy, for I, the Lord your God am holy." Then a little later comes the provision for the poor and needy, which forbids the land-proprietor to gather for himself the gleanings of the harvest; these are to be left as a provision for those who are in need.

Then follow the great injunctions which are so closely in line with the Ten Commandments, as found in Exodus xx., that they may well be called a slightly different literal, though essentially identical spiritual, version of the Decalogue. Truly it may be said that positive and negative statements are freely intermingled, but it is not possible to avoid negative commands altogether until we have risen from Sinai to Zion, and we are even today as peoples only on the road to the Messianic Era. In the face of the manifold injustices which still prevail even in the most civilized communities, the grand old prohibitions of the Mosaic Law need constantly to be resounded. Would that Sinai's thunders might once for all be hushed and our ears attuned forevermore to Zion's tender whispers; but present conditions need trumpet-tongued prophets as well as silver-tongued orators; and though the golden voice of the Messiah is the only voice which is heard in the celestial heavens, the earths of today need to be convulsed with tones of living thunder.

Let us remember, however, that always and everywhere there are at least two tones audible in the same reverberation. The undertone we are all familiar with, but the overtone we have not so often heard. Sinai's undertones are never unaccompanied by overtones. Let us listen diligently, that we may hear through the former the dulcet cadence of the latter. "Ye shall not steal nor deal falsely, nor lie one to another." If we are at the base of the mountain, we shall be awestricken when we hear those prohibitions, for they must needs strike terror into guilty hearts, for when conscience smites us with its disapproval, it does indeed make cowards of us all.

Moses and Shakespeare frequently keep very close together. But if we have ascended far up toward the mountain peak, or if we are within the mountain's heart and hear the echo of the detonating thunder as it reaches the quiet peaceful chambers of the sanctuary within, we shall not hear threatenings nor condemnations, but sweet assurances unto Israel—promises made to the holy ones that because of their love of holiness, nothing false or vile can possibly overcome them.

Though others steal, yet Israel shall be honest; though others lie, yet Israel shall be truthful; how else can Israel's mission be fulfilled as enlightener of all the families of humanity? The code of morals is surely very high, and greatly in need of enforcement today. This insists that no workman shall be defrauded of even a fraction of his hire, and that no undue respect shall be shown to the rich, nor contempt showered upon the poor; and to cap the climax of practical morality, the words must be vigorously enforced, "Thou shalt not go up and down as a tale-bearer among thy people."

Gossips are of ancient date. No literature fails to mention them, and the venerable Pentateuch especially protests against any continuance of their nefarious occupation. "Thou shalt not hate thy neighbor in thy heart," comes first as a precept, and quickly following it we read, "Thou shalt love thy neighbor as thyself." Among these superlatively grand and most important counsels are many ritual injunctions which, unless spiritually interpreted, may well be supposed to relate to other times than these; but of those we are not now called upon to speak.

Still reading Leviticus xix, we find that there is absolutely no justification therein for the ignorant supposition so often trumpeted abroad, that prior to the advent of Christianity a neighbor meant only a co-patriot or co-religionist. That such a statement is absolutely false to history, is positively proved by these words (Verse 34) : "The stranger that dwelleth with you shall be unto you as one born among you, and thou shalt love him as thyself." Those sublime words are in the King James version, and therefore have been for nearly three hundred years in the vernacular of all English speaking readers of the Bible; whence, then, can have arisen the false charge against early Judaism, that it did not counsel the lovely doctrine so touchingly illustrated by the blessed Jesus, when, after relating the incident of the Good Samaritan who helped a man not of his own race or religion, he said to all who enquired of him concerning the neighbor, *"Go thou and do likewise."*

The time is already come for a complete and thoroughly honest re-statement of Christian doctrine, and in the course of this restatement no honor need be taken from the historic Christ, for the evangelists all report him as having declared that he came to fulfill the ancient law, and God's law is fulfillable only in love. "Ye shall do no unrighteousness. Just balances, just weights shall ye have."

However important may be the "just weight" and the "just balance" in the market place, and however commendable the theology of the brusque English Unitarian who, when asked what is included in the Unitarian's creed, promptly replied, "One God, no devil and twenty shillings to the pound," as students of causation we are not content with mere external or formal morality and therefore know that one hundred cents to the dollar and sixteen ounces to the pound weight can never meet the full requirements of the moral law which inveighs against secret hate and insists upon open love.

It is always pitiable on the twenty-second of February to hear simply that George Washington never told a lie, for if the eulogist who is making the anniversary speech says no more than that, some wag may well enquire, "Was he dumb, sir?" and thereby create a boisterous outburst of laughter in a popular assembly. "Washington always told the truth," is a good introduction to a panegyric, and if the theme be well developed, any orator of average ability can quickly rise to heights of real sublimity when describing the character of a true hero, of whom it has been proudly said that he was first in peace and in the affection of his countrymen.

When in "Looking Backward" Edward Bellamy took occasion to remark that by the close of the twentieth century the Ten Commandments might no longer be employed in their present largely negative form, some doughty champions of the letter who do not seem to have caught much of the spirit of the Decalogue, assailed Bellamy for having spoken disrespectfully of the Mosaic Law.

About 1890 when "Looking Backward" was the literary sensation of the hour, we gave a course of lectures in San Francisco on "Old and New Sociology" which attracted very large audiences and in which we boldly said that Bellamy could fearlessly confront Moses; yea, that he could stand unabashed in the presence of the God of Moses, if his chief offense had been re-translating the Commandments and telling the children of the present day that a hundred years hence in synagogues and churches they might hear, "Thou shalt be honest," and "Thou shalt bear true witness concerning thy neighbor," in place of the old phrases which counsel us against the practices of theft and lying, which we may well hope will have become obsolete and forgotten at a time when regenerated Boston shall have long since abolished the Charlestown jail and converted every North End slum into a district fully as beautiful as the present highly lauded Back Bay district. The letter of the law is often called the burdensome yoke of the Torah. Nothing has served during recent years to bring the folly of extreme literalism more prominently before the novel-reading and theatre-frequenting populace than Israel Zangwill's highly dramatic story, "The Children of the Ghetto," for beautiful, saintly, heroic, almost divine, and withal exquisitely true to real life, though the character of "Rabbi Shemuel" undoubtedly is, the fanatical mistake of a too literal interpretation of the law concerning a divorce which follows no real marriage, but only a farcial substitute, is plainly evident to every honest casuist.

We can truly admire devotion to ideals and the brave spirit of self-sacrifice for the sake of principle, but fanaticism unfortunately is blear-eyed. It confounds superstition with conviction, and does not rest on the rocky foundation of abiding truth, but only on the slippery sand of ever-changing legalism.

The Ninth Commandment seems to many people apparently no more than a simple protest against lying, for the bearing of false witness is assuredly the telling of some untruth; but from a metaphysical viewpoint the precept reaches immeasurably deeper than the tongue. We should never refrain from embracing an opportunity to declare that it soon becomes impossible to altogether control the tongue if the thoughts which lead on to speech, are permitted to roam and revel in fields of error or revenge.

The entire tragedy of "Othello" is the Shakespearian protest against giving ear to slander. "Emilia," the sweet, pure-minded woman, has no inclination to believe in "Desdemona's" guilt, but the invention of the treacherous "Iago" is accepted as truth by "Othello," because this "Moor of Venice" has permitted the bitter seed of jealousy or foul suspicion to take root in his too impassioned spirit.

It is only a very short and easy step from listening to slander, to repeating it, and an equally brief and simple step from repeating what may or may not be true to inventing what is unquestionably false. How piteous must be the mental state of those poor simpletons who think they are doing the cause of virtue a service by dwelling upon every report of alleged transgression and blackening their neighbors' reputations in the fond hope that they are downing vice thereby. It would be uncharitable, and perhaps unjust also, to accuse every scandal monger of a deliberate desire to injure others or to build up self upon the ruins of another's downfall, but it is indeed difficult to believe that slander and detraction can be animated by any real wish to serve the cause of honor or purity.

We know that in some respects we are open to the charge of being "extremists," and it may be one of our extremisms to protest most vigorously against giving ear to vituperation; but so great is the wrong done to the innocent, and so many are the malicious lies spread and multiplied by heeding slanderous tales, that we are willing to be counted among those who contend that no accusation against anyone should be heeded by anyone who wishes to excel as a genuine spiritual healer.

What sort of spectacle do "reformers" exhibit to the world when backbiting one another? How can any intelligent person expect the cause of universal peace and arbitration to be truly promoted so long as the worst possible motives are attributed to those who have not yet learned a more excellent way, and are therefore still engaged in the unrighteous course of warfare? Is it reasonable to hope that intelligent penetrative intellects will feel disposed to ally themselves with new organizations (which often promise much but accomplish little) so long as the worst elements from which they hoped to flee when they cut loose from ancient institutions, are seen to grow and thrive in each new-fangled seminary?

There may be conferences, conventions, convocations without limit in the avowed interest of "new," "progressive," "higher," "advanced," "metaphysical" and all other kinds of thought, but if the milk of human kindness be absent from the proffered banquet, all the intellectual dainties on the bountifully spread board will fail to hold, even should they succeed in attracting genuine whole-souled truth-seekers to the novel feast.

Vegetarianism and anti-vivisectionism are presumably outcomes of very tender feeling, and have for their principal object the humanizing and softening of the human race; yet only too often do we find the published utterances of vegetarians and anti-vivisectionists just as belligerent as was the stupid condemnation of men in general which used to characterize quite a considerable percentage of speeches and tracts devoted to the excellent cause of equal suffrage. "Oh, how they quarreled at the peace meeting" provokes a laugh naturally, because of the absurd incongruity of the situation; but we who are seeking to truly advance the cause of peace and good-will among the nations of the earth must take a more serious view of so hideous an anomaly than to laugh at it.

How, in the name of reason, are we going to put down war by stirring up the fierce passions of mutual hostility which alone make conflict possible? We most earnestly feel that we are helping to fulfill a divine mission whenever we protest that such measures as border on the fringe of a breach of the Ninth Commandment must be overcome by the adoption of a new and living way of salvation vs. condemnation. Let it once be known that scolding does not right wrongs or sweeten dispositions, and once let it be admitted that to scatter evil is not to destroy it, then we shall soon be well on the road to the accomplishment of those great and glorious reforms which now loom large in our ideal horizons, and which we should all co-operate to actualize as quickly as possible.

To encourage slander or evil-speaking of any sort is to countenance far more lying than most people seem to suppose. The only strictly safe course is to turn a totally deaf ear to all damaging reports which may be brought to us. It is no rebuke to a slanderer to appear shocked and to exclaim, "Oh; you don't say so!" or "I never could have believed it!"

Drastic treatment is needed for the vilifier, and no drastic measure is so effective as to let the scandal monger plainly see that we look with contempt on every foul report or unclean insinuation. Practitioners of mental healing are powerless to effect any real improvement in moral conditions, so long as they make pictures of immorality and gaze upon these in their own subjective consciousness.

No wandering boy is ever led home as a repentant prodigal because somebody sang "Where is my wandering boy tonight?" but millions of wanderers can be drawn home by such fathers as the gracious man in the story of the prodigal son, who was out on the road ready to receive and welcome his son whenever he put in, an appearance. Such sentences as "Once he was pure" and "Tell him with all his blight I love him still," are sickly ebulitions of maudlin sentiment, not strong suggestions which truly help the weak and faltering to resist temptation or grow strong to conquer it in future if in an hour of weakness they may have ignorantly yielded to a tempter.

If you give a boy or girl a good reputation to live up to, even though the child may not yet fully deserve it, it surely serves as a beacon to lure the youthful mind to nobler attainments, while a bad reputation to live down to, is the greatest curse which a growing character can possibly have to contend against. Many supposedly pious people pry about, watching every movement of the people upon whom they spy, and then report the most shameful tales, usually highly exaggerated, even when (which is but seldom) there is any actual foundation for the story in demonstrable fact.

A young man, five feet nine inches in height, about twenty-two years of age, wearing a light overcoat, was seen going into a saloon in a dim light; straightway a mother, whose son would answer to that vague general description, was told that her darling boy, the idol of her heart, was fast becoming a confirmed drunkard, gambler, or something else disgraceful. The wretch who told the mother this was a "good pious deacon," or one of the superlatively sanctified "oyster-and-ice-cream-women," without whose valuable assistance many a struggling church would go to pieces. Because "dear Mrs. Smeethe" or "pious Mr. Broone" has said this horrible thing it is accepted as true; therefore poor confiding "Mrs. Jones'" heart is broken. Of course, it is all in vain that "Charlie Jones," when charged with breaking his widowed mother's heart, protests, "It must have been some other fellow who resembles me, for I was out of town on business for the firm which employs me on the evening in question." Any confession of innocence on "Charlie's" part is but a fresh arrow thrust into his mother's lacerated side, for in her distorted Smeethe & Broone obsessed vision, this is but a proof that her "fallen" boy (once so virtuous) is a liar as well as a drunkard, a gambler, and heaven (rather hell) only knows what else that is most terrible.

False witness would soon become extinct, lying would soon sink into innocuous desuetude, if there were more members in the holy congregation of "Deaf Adders" when scandal is on the breeze. But, say many, some one surely does wrong in the world or no outrages could be perpetrated. Verily, such is the case, but guilty Ester-hazy and Paty du Clam, not innocent Alfred Dreyfus, bring railing accusations. The accuser, not the accused is usually the culprit; it will be a happy day for morals when the world awakes to the acknowledgement of this certainty.

Lies are told to cover offenses; cowardice prompts offenders to shift blame in hope of escaping punishment. God's judgments are certainly not man's judgments, for man looks only on the surface, while God is the supreme reader of all hearts. A boy or girl at school spills some ink and stains a desk or carpet. Fear of the punishment which will surely follow either detection or confession causes many a timid, shrinking child to search for some one on whom to throw the blame, and as animals are dumb (so far as human language is concerned) a cat or dog serves as an efficient scapegoat. "Please, teacher, the cat got onto the table and overturned the ink," sounds plausible, so poor pussy gets a vicarious thrashing and the poor blind teacher mumbles the scripture, "Be sure your sin will find you out;" but because of her lack of penetrativeness some child has taken a first lesson in the iniquitous doctrine of vicarious punishment.

Penalties are frequently altogether out of proportion to offenses; because of this many a trembling weakling accuses an innocent person who cannot well defend himself, not out of deliberate malice, but solely in order to escape unreasonable, though not entirely unmerited, punishment. Such chastisement or correction as may suffice to lead a child to avoid mistakes in future is kindly and remedial, but wise loving reproof never engenders falsehood because it serves to develop the sublime spirit embodied in the beautiful character of "Feraz" in Marie Corelli's marvelous romance, "The Soul of Lilith" in which a highly estimable and loveable young man is represented as praying that he may receive his full share of all needed chastisement.

Falsehood cannot stand in the presence of truth. No brazen-faced effrontery can outgaze the calm, searching glance of thoroughly truthful eyes. The teacher who can truly affirm, "I always know the truth when I hear it," is one whose influence for good among young people will prove boundless. Tale-bearing and listening to talebearers is quite sufficient to render any legitimate or reliable development of clairvoyance or psychometry impossible, for the *subself* (more correctly *superself*) which is the seat of psychic perceptiveness, is never known or heeded by those who depend upon exterior means of information concerning the characters of those around them.

Concerning references, testimonials, etc., etc., there is nothing so encouraging to falsehood as to place dependence upon what may be easily manufactured spuriously. So called "gilt-edged" or "A 1" references are snares and pitfalls for the unwary, but so blind are many to all sense of character delineation at first hand, that they positively encourage deception in all its forms simply by their own stupidity in failing to observe palpable indications.

Spiritualists often raise a great cry over pretenders in their ranks, but fraud continues to flourish in many places just because some one else's word *pro* or *con* is taken in nearly every instance. Psychical Research Societies are capable of doing really valuable work by pursuing investigations along lines of dispassionate scientific examination, but not even Crookes, James, Hyslop, Hodgson, or any other honored name is sufficient to vouch for evidence save such as these capable men have themselves individually accumulated.

We do not mean to imply that evidential testimony is useless; far from it; but we do maintain that in order to become true scientists, we must learn to use our individual faculty of discernment, thereby culturing the prophetic faculty which inheres in every one of us. To simply decry lying and false swearing will never put these noxious weeds to death, because the people who indulge most in these abominations are the least heroic in the community, and in consequence of their lack of moral feeling they are not reached by simple condemnation of an offense against social order. But once let those culprits know that it is all in vain that they utter falsehoods, then even simple self-interest will lead them to take the first step toward moral growth,—discontinuance of the pernicious practices in which they formerly indulged.

False witness is often borne rather to shield an offender than for the malicious end of condemning the innocent. Cowardice, and nothing really worse than cowardice, lies at the root of an immense amount of untruthful testimony, and a coward only needs to be assured that his mendacity can prove of no avail in the face of a penetrating spiritual vision which knows innocence wherever it sees it, and therefore cannot believe guilt to be at the door of one who is offenseless.

It does absolutely no good to punish people in an arbitrary way, for telling falsehoods, because such punishments as are generally meted out by irascible persons (particularly to children) only serve to encourage clandestine manoeuverings to accomplish wrong and evade detection. Moral mental treatment suggests to whoever has spoken falsely, "you love truth inwardly, you can and you will speak truth and truth only henceforward. You love your neighbor even as you love yourself, and you know that all human interests are served by truth, and by truth only."

It is never necessary to confine oneself, when giving mental treatment, to any rigid form of printed or remembered words, but the above terse sentences may serve as a guide to many who are earnestly endeavoring to lead children (and adults also) out of the quagmire of falsehood on to the lofty eminence of unsullied truth. Love of truth must precede speaking truth, therefore the moral educator alone can exert a decided influence in ridding the world of the bitter curse of evil speaking which is the fruitful source of unmeasured misery.

"I consecrate all my vocal organs to the service of unsullied truth," is a very helpful affirmation. Any such mental ejaculation will be found in numberless instances of priceless value in aiding travelers toward the hill of Zion to reach the lightcrowned summit, standing on which they can jubilantly exclaim "We all love to speak the truth, ever one concerning his neighbor."

LECTURE ELEVEN.

THE TENTH COMMANDMENT.

"Thou Shalt Not Covet Anything That Is Thy Neighbor's."

We have now reached the crown of the Decalogue and are called upon to consider a commandment, the import of which is so vast that its purely spiritual or metaphysical character is clearly self-evident. The other nine commandments may be taken by literalists to have reference only, or chiefly, to external conduct, such as is comprised in speech and action, but covetousness is no outward or visible offense. It is of the inner nature and pertains to thought and affection, not to word and action. It is, therefore, a secret sin, and as such frequently passes unnoticed and uncondemned, when offenses of all overt characters are speedily denounced by sticklers for the Law's literal observance. When we read the thrilling words in one of the New Testament epistles "He who breaks the Law at one point is guilty of all," we feel disposed to think that the writer of that searching indictment must have had the Tenth Commandment especially in mind.

It is always some secret offense which undermines virtue most completely, because it carries on its stealthy occupation of destruction unsuspected and unmolested. We are not bringing a railing accusation against those who sin in thought, for oftentimes they know not that mental iniquities are of any serious consequence. Owing to the intense and truly barbaric devotion still paid to mere externals, children are allowed to grow up, as a rule, without anything approaching an adequate idea of the importance of thought as a fashioner of external conditions. "As a man thinketh in his heart so is he," clearly means not only that God sees and reads the heart, and that all spiritual judgments are passed from interior discernment, instead of from outward observation, but additionally to this, that every secret unsuspected thought makes for outward expression as it weaves its characteristic clothing. and renders inevitable through the incessant working of the law of correspondences, an exterior body which is in the likeness of the formative mind.

Leaving the strictly ethical or severely moral aspects of the sin of covetousness, we ought, as scientific thinkers, to dwell much upon the effect of thought, not only upon bodily health but equally upon ulterior circumstances. Twenty or fewer years ago when the "craze" for mental healing was in its youthful bloom all over the United States far too many people were carried away with a superficial theory of treatment which began and ended with the hope that, in some mysterious manner, a panacea might be found for physical suffering in some strange system of thought and practice which delighted, while it bewildered, the multitude by its novelty and incomprehensibility. Thousands of men and women paid large prices for a course of instruction consisting of twelve lessons in Christian Science, and then went to work to heal everybody who was ailing, and we all know that great success and also pitiable failures have been chronicled in their history.

Today there is great interest manifest in treatments for overcoming poverty as well as sickness, and many metaphysical teachers and practitioners do not hesitate to say that poverty and sickness are all of a piece, so that if one can be cured so can the other. There is logical historic continuity revealed in this special interest in two quite distinct, but closely related, realms of mental action—conquest over sickness and over poverty. Great significance attaches to the fact that it was first sickness, then poverty which people sought to vanquish by mental methods, for we must first become superior, within ourselves, to the action of adverse conditions, before we are in any way ready to control environments.

Covetousness is one of the greatest imaginable drawbacks to success in every line of enterprise, because the covetous person is perpetually looking outside of self and wishing to appropriate what is now in the possession of some other human being. Strong, searching, teaching, couched in the plainest possible language is specially needed on this subject. Straws show in which way the current is flowing, and very conspicuous and suggestive "straws" are frequently in evidence as we listen to the casual remarks of persons who are in no way malicious, but who are continually wishing that they possessed something which is now in the keeping of another. It is pitiable to observe the crying injustice in the world, which no one seems to know how to rectify, unless it be a few thoroughgoing metaphysicians who are looked upon as heartless oftentimes by screeching and gushing fraternities, because they insist that no screaming against present inequality will ever bring about a condition of equality. However equal we may be essentially and potentially, we are at present extremely unequal in our grasp upon great fundamental principles of universal law and order. Whenever one covets what another holds he accuses himself of incompetency or inefficiency, because he confesses to wanting something he is unable to fashion, evolve, or lawfully attract. There is no niggardliness in the scheme of Nature or in the Nature of Things; no great teacher has ever taught parsimony or counseled envy.

We read in the gospels that when several thousands of men, women, and children were hungry, Jesus multiplied bread and fish to such an extent that when every one had been fully satisfied twelve basketfuls of overplus were collected by disciples of the great wonder-worker who had thus marvelously supplied a multitude with sustenances even in a desert.

We know well enough that "higher criticism" seeks to effectually dispose of the letter of every alleged miracle, and leaves only the spiritual lesson which a significant fable or poem may convey. We have no quarrel with "higher critics" in this respect, because we are as fully aware as they that the letter of an ancient story is of no great value at best to the people of today. At the same time we see no reason for denying the possibility of even literal occurrences not necessarily supernatural, but so unusual as to appear such to the spectators of mysterious phenomena. A widespread foolish tendency to limit Nature is a source of endless controversy and dispute.

Modern Psychism is throwing new light on ancient magic and alchemy, and we are beginning to strip the mysterious very largely of its long-time covering of out-and-out supernaturalism. But our immediate task is not to enter deeply into the ever fruitful topic of "miracles" but only to show how far we may, by eradicating covetousness, attain to a healthy happy estate of (at least) comparative opulence, instead of remaining fixed in the chronic wretchedness of hopeless poverty in which so many well-meaning people are held today.

Covetousness is in itself sufficient to account for a very large percentage of all the non-success which now afflicts the race. "I wish I had her hair," says some innocent maiden gazing out of a window onto a street along which is passing a radiant girl whose magnificent tresses are freely exposed to the view of all beholders. The girl behind the window has no intention of surreptitiously depriving the object of her admiration of her luxuriant hair, but she is, all unconsciously, weakening her own thin locks by throwing a portion of her force or energy into the foolish and anti-social desire to possess some other maiden's tresses. As years pass on it is some one else's house, carriage, position, friends, reputation, or even husband, which may be coveted, and the poor coveter, all unknowingly, is depleting her own exchequer and wasting her opportunities of legitimate enrichment by hankering after something belonging to another, instead of setting studiously to work to build up her own self-conscious womanhood to the extent of drawing to herself everything necessary to her health, happiness and usefulness. The wildest crimes are often committed as final consequences of covetousness; but even when no criminal act is even contemplated, there is a constant drain of vitality resulting from the wish to take from others instead of so building up oneself that the magnet within shall attract all that is desirable.

Nations begin to grow weak internally the very instant they begin to covet the territory of other nations. Discontent and atrophy, together with many flagrant immoralities, quickly result from seeking to subdue other countries in place of building up one's native land or the country of one's adoption. America has, in our opinion, recently made some serious blunders, and though we bring no fierce accusations against the present or any past administration, we do not hesitate to say, that if a spirit of desire to annex unwilling peoples shall be fostered in the United States, it will prove a thorn in Columbia's side, and hinder her advancement toward her predestined goal of internal wealth and consummate civilization. Though it seems that some children are born with greater momentum than others, consequently some achieve greatness in any line more readily than do others, there is enough vitality in every one of us to bear us forward to a very considerable measure of success, if we would but give up, once for all, the old wretched spirit of dependence upon fate, luck, chance or fortune, which is too many people's evil genius, though a supposed divinity.

The great commercial success of the Jewish people is very largely attributable to their very general conviction that they have, within themselves, unusual ability to control finance and lead in scientific, literary, and art directions. Anti-Semitic agitators and their dupes are a set of weaklings who feel deeply their own innate powerlessness to fairly compete with the Sons of Israel, so they must tell falsehoods, fling mud and call a man a "parasite" who has a larger measure of self-confidence than their petty selves. Jews are often oppressive and not always amiable, but they are on the whole self confident, persevering and industrious, and seek far more to build themselves up than to pull their neighbors down. The clannishness, of which the typical "Ghetto" Jew is constantly accused, is, in itself, a mark of strength, for it stands for co-operation and reciprocity *vs* mutual hatred and disdain.

No body of people is wholly free from covetousness, so there are unsuccessful and puny Jews as well as Gentiles, but Israel's heritage has ever been the Torah of which the Decalogue is the veritable quintessence. Scientifically speaking, every thought or desire fixed upon some ulterior object, now in the possession of another, sets up a discordant vibration within the system of the one who covets, and the effect of all discord is destructive to the very fibre and tissue of the interiors of the human organism.

Music can be employed most successfully as a healing agent by any strong healthy musician who feels harmony and then reproduces it externally. Energy is lost, strength is frittered away by permitting, even in the smallest degree, the injurious thought that your success means some one else's failure, or that some one else's victory signals your defeat. There is a physiological accompanying a psychological deterioration continually going on within the gambler; all games of chance are weakening because they engender the hope that something may be obtained by chance instead of by honest effort. All great prophets in olden times rebuked high officials in church and state indiscriminately. Josiah found the grossest wickedness in the highest places and scrupled not to say so. We must therefore not be surprised to find that "holy" places are often nurseries of evil and incubators of the worst vices which infest society. What harm is there in a raffle for a fancy quilt or picture? is a question frequently put to us by students. There is no actual dishonesty or unfair dealing provided the raffle is honorably conducted, but at its mildest, or in its least offensive form, it inculcates a doctrine diametrically opposed to the higher social eth-

ics. Why should I want ninety-nine people beside
myself to pay one shilling, or twenty-five cents, toward
an object worth 5 pounds or $25, which I hope to carry
home for the adornment of my private dwelling, when I
have done nothing whatever to earn that twenty-five
dollar article, except put twenty-five cents, a single shilling, as ninety-nine others have done, into a lottery
ticket? It is true that everybody in the hundred takes
an equal chance, but we cannot build up noble character or successful business on a stable foundation so long
as we believe in chance. "That's just my luck;" "Oh,
you are a lucky dog," and many similar expressions,
seemingly innocent, must all be vetoed before we can set
to work to build from foundation to attic, or work
from centre to circumference in the evolution of prosperity. Every desire to get something for nothing
weakens moral fibre and works against even financial
opulence. The "poor relation," or the idle dependent
relative in any household, quickly becomes degenerate,
so do all people who are continuously worked for by
others, who never think it proper to expect these polite
paupers to work honorably for themselves.

Ingratitude is not always so base as it appears; this is
instanced in the pathetic incident of Beethoven and his
nephew. To pay a young man's gambling debts or
to bring up a girl in idleness is not kindness, nor is it
charity, therefore if the one who has been immorally
trained, turns upon the trainer with ingratitude, if cen-
sure must be meted out at all, both sides must be entitled to a portion of it,—though to surface observers one
looks the embodiment of all kindness and the other of
all unrighteousness. If Henrik Ibsen had studied psychology more deeply he would have been less pessimistic
in his dramas, and even as it is, his saddest plays are
only gloomy commentaries upon the true old words,
"whatever we sow we reap."

Covetousness saps energy because it diverts the stream
of vital force within the individual into an extraneous,
therefore into an alien channel. If you are constantly
gazing upon the house across the way and wishing it were
yours, instead of continuing to be the property of its
present owner, your psychic energy crosses the street
and accumulates on the other side of the road; if you
keep this up for any considerable length of time or
indulge the practice constantly, you may see your envied
neighbor growing steadily wealthier while your prospects for ever owning a home of your own are steadily
dwindling. If on the other hand you reason thus with
yourself: "The man opposite has a good home and I am
glad he has one, but I am going to have a good one,

too," you will be positively encouraged by his success, and your reasoning faculties remaining unbeclouded (growing indeed constantly more vigorous) you will soon begin to take practical steps to own your own cottage or maybe your own mansion.

Successful people are self-centred, no matter what line of work they may pursue, and a self-centred person is far too busy with his own employments to fritter away time and energy in coveting his neighbor's goods. Churches are often covetous, but whenever covetousness invades a religious congregation, dissensions spring up, finances decline, and there is a general feeling of dissatisfaction and desire on the part of the members to seek some other affiliation, while strangers visiting the building are repelled instead of attracted by an "atmosphere," no matter how handsome the building, how fine the music, or how eloquent the sermon.

A typical *Dr. Wolf* preaches to full pews, but *Dr. Bear* addresses a glittering array of nearly empty benches. Straightway *Dr. Bear* begins to argue that *Dr. Wolf* is his *enemy*, for to his distorted mental vision, if *Dr. Wolf* could only be removed or silenced the "lupine" congregation would flock to *Bruin's* ministrations. Nothing of the sort, sir; you are totally mistaken. Every preacher draws his own following, and there are many who would absent themselves from preaching altogether if *Dr. Wolf* retired, unless a successor filled his place who gave the public the same sort of mental nourishment. Popular preachers are not popular because they preach in certain definite localities. Bishop Phillips Brooks was not listened to by constant multitudes because he preached in Boston, or because his pulpit was in Trinity Church, Copley Square, for he was followed by crowds wherever he went, so much so that when church-wardens in several places complained to him of the paucity of church attendance, he answered guilelessly, "I think churches are very well attended, for wherever I go I find a large congregation." People did not go in crowds to listen to Rev. M. J. Savage when he was in Boston because he preached in an old church in West Newton street, which has since been demolished, for no sooner did that brilliant Unitarian go to New York than the old edifice in Boston became nearly empty, and was soon disposed of to another denomination, which very soon erected a new edifice on the site of the antiquated structure so long a celebrated temple.

For thirty years Dr. Joseph Parker drew vast crowds to the City Temple, Holborn Viaduct, but Londoners are not particularly fond of going to church in that locality on Sundays, for it is an essentially commercial work-a-day center, and should a less attractive pulpit orator than Mr. Campbell have taken Dr. Parker's place, it is very doubtful whether a large building in that locality could be even half filled at every service. Dr. Emil Hirsch in Chicago is the attraction at Sinai Temple, and were he to accept an offer to go to New York or any other city unless another man equally powerful and energetic should fill his place, Indiana Avenue and Twenty-second street would not continue such a very well-known liberal Jewish corner. Dr. Thomas, not McVicker's Theatre, in the same city was the attraction in the heart of a business section for many years on Sundays. These illustrations are extremely trite, but they are very timely, for they serve (among hundreds of others) to convince every reflective intellect, that to covet another's position is the act of a consummate simpleton. Could you fill another's place even were you permitted to occupy it? is a burning leading question. If we are wise we do not wish to be burdened with other people's duties, obligations or responsibilities, for we have quite enough to do to attend to our own engagements which are sufficiently onerous and continually increasing.

Helen Wilmans, in "A Conquest of Poverty," has preached finely on the Tenth Commandment, though perhaps she has not even mentioned it, but in all her exhortations to her readers to develop their individual selfhood, she delivers a homily from the text, "Thou shalt not covet." Shallow scribbling concerning Bible inconsistencies has actually reached the point of imbecility when a writer has said that Paul, when writing to the Corinthians concerning spiritual gifts, directed people to covet them. What laughter such folly must occasion among theological students, to say nothing of professors of the Greek language, from which an unfortunate English translation has occasionally been made. Should this discourse fall into the hands of any one who is totally ignorant of the meaning of the disputed passage (I Cor. xii, 31) let him remember when he reads it, that "to desire earnestly," or "seek earnestly to obtain," would be a fair rendering of the original, and is in perfect consonance with the whole tenor of the cluster of chapters concerning spiritual endowments in which that particular verse is found. (Vide Revised Version for approximately accurate rendering.) But even had so illustrious a man as Paul the apostle counseled covetousness, it would only have proved the inferiority of some of the teachings of Paul to the contents of the Mosaic Decalogue. It would be a fool's errand to run in search of lingual inaccuracies in the New Testament epistles wherewith to bolster up the divine Law, which needs no bolstering. Let us all start out with a new resolve—a sacred determination never to permit the slightest particle of covetousness to invade the sanctuary of our thoughts. Think how blessed it would be if every inhabitant of the world should arise tomorrow morning, free from all desire to take aught from the possessions of a neighbor, but each one appear inflamed with the ardent fire of true aspiration prompting each to become great, noble, successful, honorable, through well directed individual industry. Reciprocity (not competition) is the life of honest business. Universal co-operation alone will merge the many Trusts of today into one great Trust in the future, in which all the inhabitants of the earth will be mutually interested. Bellamy and other nineteenth-century prophets caught glimpses of the Golden Age to come, but "Nationalist Clubs" though they started with a great flourish of trumpets, soon became absorbed in other enterprises, because the monopolistic spirit was not absent from their internal management. We have to be content with the "boss," because many of us believe greatly in the power of the boss and (secret out) we should like to be bosses ourselves.

Bossism feeds upon people who wish they could boss others while they particularly dislike to be bossed themselves. False standards everywhere are the causes of the prevalent unrest and deep-seated misery which it is the province of Spiritual Science to overcome; not by aping any false measures externally in vogue, but by steadfastly adhering to those sublime interior principles of action for which all genuine metaphysicians unreservedly must stand. "Thou shalt not covet" can be Zionized as can all the other Commandments, and when from the heights of Zion we hear the new interpretation of the old command, there shall ring in our ears this blest enunciation, "Thou shalt ever rejoice in thy neighbor's welfare and thou shalt understand in thy heart that humanity is one even as God is ONE."

Whatsoever blesses thy neighbor blesses thee, and whatever advanceth thy interest equally advanceth the welfare of all thy brethren. In the foregoing sentence the essential spirit of the 10th Commandment is sufficiently epitomized.

LECTURE TWELVE.

ON THE HEIGHT OF ZION.

"The Law Shall Go Forth from Zion."

In this concluding lecture we shall attempt to restate in simple graphic language a few of those fundamental postulates of Divine Science which we have expounded in some slight measure during the previous eleven discourses. We started in lecture one, with a general statement regarding the plan and scope of such revelation as we may find accessible in our own day and related to our own life.

We then proceeded in ten consecutive discourses to treat the Commandments one by one, not by any means adhering strictly to their literal meaning, though that could never be ignored; now we come to divine realization when our sole endeavor is to construct and not destroy. No Christian commentator seems shocked at the boldness of Paul where he says, "We are not under the law but under grace" and "the law was a schoolmaster to bring us to the Christ." When descanting upon the glories of the Hill of Zion the same writer says, "We are not come unto Sinai" and then contrasts the burning, quaking mount with the "assembly and church of the first-born, whose names are written in Heaven."

Though conviction may compel us to differ radically from much teaching which has long passed muster as evangelical, we are not in the least disposed to protest against a single line of what we conceive to have been the apostle Paul's intention when he wrote those stirring poetic words which have caused him to be regarded by many as the real founder of acknowledged Christianity.

Henry Wood, in "Victor Sirenus" has given us a picture of Saul of Tarsus, the intrepid pupil of the eminent rabban Gamaliel, which shows that fiery character to have been originally a fanatical, as well as an ultra-orthodox Jew. The seventy elders constituting the Sanhedrim of whom Gamaliel was one, were no doubt, at that period in history, far more liberal and gentle than their traducers have represented, but though Henry Wood is always a polished writer, never indulging in diatribe or harsh invective, we consider that in *Victor Sirenus*, he has been unnecessarily severe in dealing with the conventional Judaism of the time of Saul of Tarsus.

There have always been several parties among the Jews. All are familiar with the names of Pharisees and Saducees which occur so frequently in the gospels, and all scholars speak of Essenians or Essenes as a third and by no means inoperative, though comparatively silent party. The venerable Rabbi Wise, for many years President of the Union Theological Seminary in Cincinnati, says that Jesus and his immediate disciples were Pharisees, and being on the inside as members of the Pharisaic body were more vehement in their denunciations of its hypocrisies than any outside agitators would have been.

Such a man as Prof. Geo. Herron in his striking books on the present social and industrial state of civilization says far stronger things concerning churches and colleges than are usually uttered by people who have never been professors in either and who therefore only glean from hearsay what they report concerning ecclesiastical and academic life.

It is only a Savonarola, or one of like spirit with him, who can scourge the church internally and bid it repent of its corruptions and return to its first love so that it be not swept from the face of the earth because of its transgressions. The greatest lesson obviously to be learned from the story of the conversion of Saul into Paul needed by the people of today, substantially reads thus: Give heed no longer to the external voices of priests and magistrates, but go thy own way from Damascus to Jerusalem and on the road between those cities thou shalt see a light and hear a voice, and if thou art wise thou wilt turn toward that light, and reply to that voice, and thou wilt say unto the divine speaker who is breathing fresh knowledge of truth to thee, "Speak, Lord, for thy servant heareth," and "Lord, what wilt thou have me to do."

Outward voices are conflicting and, though ecclesiastics may stickle for uniformity, unity is utterly impossible where conscience and reason are alike fettered and one cannot or dare not say his soul is his own. "This is exactly what it is not," the theologian at once exclaims, "for all souls belong to God, and you are responsible to the Almighty for your soul which is not your own, but your Creator's." If that were all that theologians told us, we should not rebel against their dictum, but they very quickly proceed to build up a sophistical edifice erected by subtle casuistry, in which they seek to imprison every would-be free-thinker on religious subects. For, say they, "Free thought is abominable and heresy is the worst of all offenses." The world's thinkers have always brought a scathing indictment against prelatical hierarchies, accusing them of subverting morals and making the word of God of none effect through vain traditions.

We cannot as ethical teachers, sympathize in the least degree with systems which exalt creed above deed, and make salvation depend upon belief in dogmas and compliance with ordinances, rather than upon noble, consistent, self-evolved, moral character. Society can hold together very well without priests and rituals, but it must fall to pieces if inward moral strength is lacking. English Nonconformity has developed a sturdier race of thinkers than has the Established Church of England, taking the two sections of the English population all in all. And why has this been so? Surely because ever since 1662, and even before that great historic date, the non-conforming element has been uncompromising.

Saul of Tarsus did not reject or repudiate spiritual Judaism when he began to preach "Christ and Him crucified," he only shook himself free of multiplied ancestral traditions which are to this very day the bane of Jew and Gentile equally in many places. If forms and ceremonies are regarded as optional, they are unobjectionable, for no one has a right to tell his neighbor that he shall not engage in such religious exercises as he conscientiously enjoys. Two eulogies could be pronounced on one day by the same speaker without incongruity; one on Oliver Cromwell, the other on Sir Thomas Moore, provided the panegyrist had a sufficiently broad grasp of the general subject of human nobility to enable him to duly respect the inalienable rights of the Congregationalist on the one hand, and of the Roman Catholic on the other. Every one must find God and reach Heaven in his own way. The Holy Spirit is an indwelling enlightener, not an outside teacher. The spirit within, not the institution without is the infallible guide to faith and practice, and as to the Bible, men wrote the books which compose it as they were inspired to write, but books could have no existence were it not for the mental activity of their authors.

Self reliance and reliance upon God are ultimately identical, for though there is a shallow vaunting atheism which vainly imagines that to get rid of the idea of God is to attain the very summit of human freedom, reason turns away affronted by such superficial sputtering and looks again to the idea of a Supreme Intelligence as the only solid ground of assurance that all that *is* is good, therefore in reality there can be no evil permanent in the Universe.

Christian Scientists constantly reiterate the words of Mrs. Eddy, "God is principle, not person." We prefer to say "God is principle revealed through person." Denials are always hampering; nothing so fetters the intellect or dwarfs the rising and expanding reason as to be told emphatically by some one who professes to know more than others, that something is *not* so; and though in the practical work of mental and spiritual healing, denials as well as affirmations have long occupied a prominent place, it has always been a decided part of our teaching to substitute affirmative for negative statements wherever possible.

Take for instance the old foolish mischievous practice of frightening children. Lazy, impatient, irritable parents and nurses find it quicker, and therefore easier, to slap a child, to box ears, to threaten with condign punishment some trifling offense, than they find it to reason with the little ones and point out to them the more excellent way. The reputed "Devil" can always quote scripture according to a time honored proverb. So from the book of Proverbs, Mr. Spankhard and Mrs. Earboxer profess to derive divine sanction for their egregious misconduct, "Spare the rod and spoil the child" is a trite adage but utterly misconstrued. The old Jewish idea of the "rod" was education; the Talmud in many places speaks of the dire penalties following parental neglect in the education of children.

In the twenty-third Psalm we are all familiar with the accustomed reading, "Thy rod and thy staff they comfort me." Surely no sane person supposes that comfort is to be derived from a birch rod or "cat o' nine tails," but as rod is also a *measure* and the intention of education is to enable the educated to measure things with accuracy, we can easily see that the "rod" which measures the holy city described in the Apocalypse may be identical with that rod which must not be spared in the bringing up of children.

Suicide is today a formidable question in many places. It is not helpful to tell a poor wretch that some theological dogma dooms him to an endless hell if he dares to rashly throw himself into the realms unseen. Very quickly many archbishops and other dignitaries of the church may find themselves answered in one of two ways. The one who is contemplating suicide will retort, "I don't believe in your hell anyway" or he is likely to exclaim from the pit of his wretchedness "If there be a hell in the hereafter, I don't believe it can be worse than the hell I'm in on earth already." France, which has long professed to be a Christian country, incarcerated Dreyfus for five years on Devil's Island, submitting him to the cruelest torture, though absolutely nothing had been proved against him and there have been bombastic churchmen seeking to palliate or extenuate the enormity not only of that one offense but of numerous similar offenses. Christianity as institutionalized is no gospel of good tidings for all people. It is, on the contrary, anything but delightful news for all who do not utterly submit to its arbitrary enforcements; but that esoteric doctrine which Paul promulgated and which is true Theosophy, is the soul or animating spirit of the Christian system even as it is the secret doctrine of all religions, the "mystery" of all ages by means of the knowledge of which alone can all creeds be interpreted and the internal essence of all doctrines be explained. Of one thing the sceptic may well rest assured, *viz.*, that with the decay of the doctrines of exoteric religion scepticism will not be accepted as a substitute for religion. Agnosticism may be a step, but as Felix Adler said long since, it is no finality. Psychical Research is not simply the "fad" of the hour, it is a conspicuous form taken by a deep and ineradicable determination on the part of earnest truth-seekers to peer below the surface and discover *sub* and *super* planes of human consciousness. Absolute fearlessness is essential to spiritual growth, but by fearlessness we do not mean rashness or incautiousness. A thoroughly fearless person is the only one who truly understands what the "fear of the Lord" really means, for such a one alone can understand the spiritual import of the lines, "With head erect and conscience clear, fear God and know no other fear." "The fear of man bringeth a snare." "Fear hath torment," "Perfect love casteth out fear," and many other equally well-known quotations suggest a dual line of reasoning on the part of the master-spirits of humanity; discrepancies may appear on the surface of their language, but contradictions in sentiment there are none. Fear in its noble ethical sense is simply reverence.

To revere God is to be animated with the deepest possible respect or reverence for righteousness, a word, which like holiness and a few others of equally universal import, means nothing short of all that we feel to be good, pure, noble and worthy, consequently worshipful.

True worship is acknowledgement of worth. Worship, adoration, or veneration (use which term we may) signifies devotion to an ideal; we are not terror-stricken or affrighted, but inspired with awe in the presence of incalculable sublimity. There are lower and higher planes of human development which must be duly acknowledged, but never confounded one with the other. People speak often of Law and Gospel as though the two were totally distinct, so much so that one has to be taken away and the other substituted. Such a misconception of letter and spirit is radically false, for the spirit is within the letter; the literal shell needs only to burst open that the indwelling spirit may stand revealed. The Beatitudes are in the Commandments and verily the blessings are in the curses. In the English book of Common Prayer there is a "Commination Service" appointed to be read in churches on Ash Wednesday (the first day of Lent). This service contains a list of curses, as they are popularly termed, taken word for word from the Pentateuch. Among them are these sayings, "Cursed is he who removeth his neighbor's landmark" and "Cursed is every one who maketh the blind to go out of the way." Many gentle-hearted Christians have objected to this service, and striven for its discontinuance, some having even gone so far as to class these severe moral precepts with the altogether reprehensible damnatory clauses in the Athanasian Creed. Though willing to avow that the Beatitudes might well be substituted, we are still of the opinion that there are people even yet who may be benefitted by a recital of those tremendous words of condemnation leveled against unrighteousness. The mind which would class such strong, equitable ethical teaching with the hateful clauses in a creed which daringly condemns every unbeliever in an unfathomable mystery to endless perdition, and then inconsistently quotes Jesus, who says, "They who have done good shall go into life everlasting," must be possessed of a very feeble intellect and be singularly deficient in reasoning ability, for moral conduct and theological subtleties have not even a remote connection. If you are ready for Zion you have no further need for Sinai but if you are not yet ready for the spirit within you still need to hear the letter enunciated without.

The question is sometimes raised by modern teachers: Which are you living under, Law or Gospel? If an answer be intelligently given, it should be: According to that Law of which Gospel is the essence.

Let us now look at the Nine Beatitudes and see how they compare with the Ten Commandments.

The Sermon on the Mount presupposes prior spiritual elevation, for according to tradition it was only preached to a few disciples who had made the effort necessary to climb a steep incline to listen to it. The teacher on the hilltop begins at once with a startling declaration of supreme benediction, which when fairly translated reads, "Blessed are the petitioners for light; theirs is the kingdom of heaven."

"Blessed are the poor in spirit" is a dubious phrase which can either be made to agree in essence with the true original or can be taken as a premium placed on cowardice rather than on bravery.

"Poverty of spirit" means to many who hear of it nothing short of weak moral inefficiency, it is therefore suggestive of tame submission to existing injustice in place of sturdy uncompromising devotion to conviction at all hazards.

"Blessed are the beggars for light," which is the exact equivalent of the Greek text according to many reputable scholars, conveys a meaning exactly synchronous with the full gist of the teaching attributed in the Synoptics to the great Teacher of righteousness to whom the saying is accredited. It is easy to justify a highly ethical interpretation of the conventional reading "poor in spirit" in strict consonance with the spirit which makes for arbitration and will not sanction warfare; but no grander opening to the Sermon on the Mount has yet been suggested by a careful comparison of ancient Manuscripts than the version we have cited. Following directly upon this first blessing, we encounter a second which harmonizes entirely with it. "Blessed are they that mourn for they shall be comforted." Consolation for the distressed is the second note in the great preacher's inimitable sermon. If there be no balm of Gilead in your ministry you are a poor sermonizer indeed, for though you may sparkle and glitter, though your rhetoric and oratory may be unimpeachable, you display head without heart; you are in that case no *healer*. Without love, which is the very soul of healing ministry, you may well be likened unto sounding brass or a tinkling cymbal. The third beatitude is a conundrum to many.

"Blessed are the meek for they shall inherit the earth." The future tense of the verb must loom large in that benediction or it has no literal import; but in its deeper meaning it is a wonderfully deep-sighted declaration that the true possessors of the land are those who truly enjoy it. If one is a chronic invalid, fed on water gruel and wheeled about in a bath chair, with no capacity for enjoying the widespread beauty of natural scenery all around, there is no true advantage in owning, in a legal sense, a wide domain. Though we are advocates of Single Tax and recommend the works of Henry George to all our students, when we are drilling our classes in self-development and expounding true individuality we invariably say: Character first; possessions afterward. The greatest impediment in the way of carrying out useful and necessary reforms is the tendency, which is very strong with most people, to start at the wrong end of everything. Let's get the land first, say they, then we may set to work to develop character; to which we reply, *sophistry*. How do you propose to get anything until you have first developed that inner force which will enable you to obtain it? The lamentable failure of hundreds of noble enterprises is due entirely to the false impression so widely entertained that we must first *own* something and then *be* something, while the exact truth is that we must first *be* something, then we can proceed to own all that is desirable for us to take possession of. Much private property soon becomes a toil and burden, for just so soon as one has accumulated much more than is sufficient for use and comfort, added possessions of a personal nature only involve additional care and the expenditure of energy on trifles pertaining to the estate which could far more enjoyably, as well as profitably, be expended on higher things.

The fourth beatitude is a very searching one, "Blessed are they who hunger and thirst after righteousness for they shall be filled." The clear inference from this is that the pursuit of equity should occupy our entire energy and be the summit of our desire. Throw yourselves entirely into the work of establishing righteousness within, and righteousness without must needs appear as an inevitable result, thus will you who become filled with equity overflow with righteous emanations and be blessed centres whence the contagion of health and virtue will stream to near and far.

The fifth blessing, "Blessed are the merciful for they shall obtain mercy," is another probing utterance which does not seem to closely tally with commonplace, human experience. But when we consider so obvious a fact as echo, we cannot doubt that in the truest sense of all, we receive back to ourselves and into our own natures exactly what we are continually throwing forth to others. It would be utterly impossible for anyone to go out among resounding rocks and reverberating hills and though shouting love, truth, peace amid the solitudes, receive in response, hate, falsehood, warfare. If it be self-evident on the material plane that echo answers, as it must, giving us back precisely what we precipitate into the air; on the spiritual plane of our existence the law must needs work equally so that what we send forth in silence or in song, by word of mouth or on the currents of the unseen atmosphere by secret thinking only, must return to us even with interest and compound interest.

The sixth beatitude "Blessed are the pure in heart for they shall see God" means infinitely more than such a supposed sight of Deity as an introduction to a majestic personal ruler in the distant heavens would signify. The beatific vision or sight of God need not be associated with any anthropomorphic or other definable view of the Supreme Being, but when perfectly unsullied love shall enable us to see with clarified vision the Great Reality as good and good only, all devilish conceptions will have ceased from our beliefs concerning the essential nature of the universe and we shall come to know that good is all in all. That is not destructive atheism which only refuses to profess faith in what its professor does not understand; infidelity is a far different vice from its ecclesiastical definition, for no one is an infidel who loves truth, and no one is shut out from a perception of Deity who loves and wishes to promote the sway of righteousness. To see one God and all in God, is to be freed from all illusion, to have penetrated the veil of sense to be no longer in the *pronoas* having passed into the *adytum* of the universal temple. Perfect purity of affection is the only key to bliss ineffable.

The seventh beatitude, "Blessed are the peacemakers" is indeed a searching one, and had we opportunity we should halt long enough to deliver a lengthy lecture on this momentous sentence; but limited space necessitating the most hurried treatment of all these glorious sentences, we content ourselves with asking every reader to meditate often and deeply on the question: What is it to be a peacemaker? Were peace already made we could not be called upon to make it. Peace is the exception, not the rule, on earth at present, but if we are lovers of peace and therefore wishful to establish peace where it has not yet been established, we must be prepared to bring it into existence by dwelling in peace ourselves, even in the midst of turmoil.

The old sayng that it takes two to make a quarrel, is altogether accurate, for one person cannot quarrel much alone. Do not permit yourselves to admit into your consciousness the thought of surrounding inharmony, for every time you permit an inharmonious vibration from without to jar upon you in your sanctuary within, you have communicated with the spirit of discord, and let into your own dwelling the demon of strife you are vainly seeking to exorcise from the outside world. Peace societies do not accomplish all the good they might, because they fight against warfare instead of steadily generating a peace spirit which will quench the flames of war and lure the hearts, consciences, and minds of men and nations to seek for peace instead of continuing belligerent.

Avowed metaphysicians ought to stand boldly for peace. Published reports of squabbles in law courts between Christian Scientists only serve to convince the reasoning enquiring public that personal idolatry, no

matter whether directed to Mrs. Eddy or to any other
individual, together with making truth a proprietary
article, is entirely wrong and diametrically opposed to
the fundamentals of all pure and helpful teaching.
Litigation never settles disputes spiritually, and though
one may determine a copyright or any other legal question in a law court, no victory is gained for genuine
science by newspaper ventilation of private animosity.
Among people who do not countenance law suits, harsh
invective and mutual denunciation often do quite as
much harm as legal ruptures; Peacemakers are they who
living amid strife continue strifeless and are therefore
led imperceptibly to an understanding of the eighth
beatitude.

"Blessed are they who are persecuted for righteousness' sake for theirs is the kingdom of heaven." Close
upon this logically follows the ninth and final beatitude.

"Blessed are ye when men shall revile you and perse-
cute you and say all manner of evil against you falsely."
The strength of these two beatitudes clearly lies in the
fact that the clearest conceivable discrimination is made
between simple persecution and persecution for the sake
of righteousness. A genuine martyr is a witness to
truth, some one who stands firm for conviction's sake
against all persecution. No one is entitled to rank as
a martyr who is persecuted for peculiarity's sake, when
nothing but foolish waywardness, and perhaps utter
lack of consideration for the feelings of others has
brought reproach upon him. It can never be blessed to
be condemned for wrongs committed, but to be persecuted on account of righteousness secures the martyr's
diadem. Too many people reverse the beatitudes
utterly by saying "I should not care so much if it were
true of me," whereas to the reflective mind the fact that
it is untrue robs its sting of all poison for there is no
deadly venom which can touch our inner lives unless we
are ourselves venomous. Jesus says "Have no fear of
those who can destroy the flesh and that is all they can
do;" which clearly means that we can all afford to stand
securely in the consciousness of our integrity, regardless of how the world may wag or what the oppressor
may threaten. When we are on the height of Zion we
care no longer for the world's applause and no longer
are we afraid of its derision. Prophetlike, we have a
message to deliver, we are Heaven's spokesmen and our
reward is with the Eternal. We all need to be told of
the inevitable consequences of error until we have grown
to that elevation spiritually where we can lose sight of
all temporizing and live virtuously because we are in
love with virtue.

Here we must take leave of this mighty subject. Skeleton lessons on the Decalogue these discourses may be found, but however many suggestions of value may be contained within them, we must request every reader to remember that nothing more than a series of Lesson Helps has been within the writer's mind while hastily compiling this handbook for the people. There could not well be a more profitable supplement to this unpretentious volume than a set of original essays written by various readers, based upon something hinted at but not fully expounded in the foregoing pages.

Let this manual be provocative of thought and study and it will not circulate in vain. From Sinai to Zion is every soul's inevitable pilgrimage.

Finis.

LBFe 10

THE LIVING DECALOGUE

From *SINAI TO ZION*

BY

W. J. COLVILLE

AUTHOR OF

"Old and New Psychology," "The Law of
Correspondences Applied to Healing," "Destiny Fulfilled—Fate Conquered," "Text Books
of Mental Therapeutics," &c., &c.

CPSIA information can be obtained
at www.ICGtesting.com
Printed in the USA
LVHW022024300323
743062LV00002B/266